WRITING
FROM THE
CENTER

Also by Scott Russell Sanders

WRITING FROM THE CENTER

Scott Russell Sanders

Indiana University Press

BLOOMINGTON AND INDIANAPOLIS

First Paperback Edition 1997

The author and publisher gratefully acknowledge the following publications, in which portions of this book first appeared: "Buckeye" as Introduction to *In Buckeye Country*, ed. John Moor and Larry Smith (Huron, Ohio: Bottom Dog Press, 1994), and in *Orion*; "Beneath the Smooth Skin of America" (under the title "Recovering Our Sense of Place") in *Notre Dame Magazine*; "Sanctuary" in *The Ohio Review*; "The Common Life" in *The Georgia Review*; "Faith and Work" (under the title "Acts of Faith") in *Notre Dame Magazine*; "The Writer in the University" in *ADE Bulletin* and *AWP Chronicle*; "News of the Wild" as Introduction to the *Sierra Club Wilderness Calendar 1995*; "Voyageurs" in *The Nature of Nature*, ed. William H. Shore (New York: Harcourt Brace, 1994); "Earth, Air, Fire, and Water" (under the title "Ancient Quartet") in *Parabola*; "Writing from the Center" in *The Georgia Review*; and "Letter to a Reader" in *My Poor Elephant: 27 Male Writers at Work*, ed. Eve Shelnutt (Atlanta: Longstreet, 1992).

Manufactured in the United States of America

Library of Congress Cataloging-in-Publication Data

Sanders, Scott R. (Scott Russell), date
Writing from the center / Scott Russell Sanders.
p. cm.
Includes bibliographical references.
ISBN 0-253-32941-8 (cl.)   ISBN 0-253-21143-3 (pbk.)
1. Sanders, Scott R. (Scott Russell), date —Knowledge—Middle West. 2. Literature and society—Middle West—History—20th century. 3. Sanders, Scott R. (Scott Russell), date —Authorship. 4. Authors, American—20th century—Biography. 5. Middle West—Intellectual life. 6. Middle West—In literature. 7. Indiana—In literature. 8. Authorship. I. Title
PS3569.A5137Z475 1995
818'.5409—dc20
[B]   95-7146

3 4 5 6 01 00 99 98 97

for Wendell Berry

CONTENTS

ᆰ

PREFACE

How can one live a meaningful, gathered life in a world that seems broken and scattered? That question has haunted me for as long as I can remember. Insofar as I have found an answer, it has to do with understanding my place in marriage, family, and community—my place on earth, and ultimately in Creation. To be centered, as I understand it, means to have a home territory, to be attached in a web of relationships with other people, to value common experience, and to recognize that one's life rises constantly from inward depths. This book is about glimpsing and seeking and longing for that center, that condition of wholeness.

My home territory is southern Indiana, in the watershed of the Ohio River, and so, in writing about where I belong, I focus on the landscape and culture of the Midwest. The skies in my pages are filled with thunderstorms and red-tailed hawks, the creeks are bordered by limestone bluffs, the fields are planted in soybeans and corn, the woods are thick with grapevines and hickories. Wishing to know my place, I read its literature, to see how this region has been imagined by writers who stayed here as well as by those who moved away. Although I speak of the Midwest, my deeper subject is our need to belong somewhere with a full heart, wherever our place may be, whoever our people may be.

This is also a book about writing, about the motives and disciplines of the art that I practice day after day. There is no special virtue in writing; it happens to be my work. A dancer moving to music, a carpenter fitting a dovetail joint, a farmer judging the health of soil could tell you as much as I can about good work, the kind that draws on every bit of one's devotion and strength and skill. The rare times when I have felt perfectly balanced and whole, in work or play, have taught me what it means to live from the center.

Because I believe that we have been too intent on what divides us—men from women, this race from that, all of us from nature—I write about the ground we share. I do so with a keen awareness of the damage we have done to land, to water and air, to our fellow creatures, to our cities and towns, and to one another. While acknowledging what we have damaged or lost, I also speak of the abundant resources in nature, in our human inheritance, and in ourselves that might enable us to live more caringly and joyfully. I tell about canoeing on a flooded river, walking in the woods, baking bread with my daughter, remodeling a kitchen with my son, meeting my father after his death, drawing a map, composing a sentence. Whatever the subject, I find hope in the land's resilience and the mind's reach.

The more attentively I dwell in my place, the more I am convinced that behind the marvelous, bewildering variety of things there is one source. I do not pretend to know how much of my conviction arises from genuine insight, how much from longing. The essays in this book are twelve expeditions in search of that unifying, vivifying source.

Bloomington, Indiana

Nothing can grow unless it taps into the soil.

—William Carlos Williams

The human heart is local and finite, it has
roots, and if the intellect radiates from it,
according to its strength, to greater and greater
distances, the reports, if they are to be gathered
up at all, must be gathered at the center.

—George Santayana

Often one has the impression that the
personal psyche is running round this central
point like a shy animal, at once fascinated
and frightened, always in flight, and yet
steadily drawing nearer.

—Carl Jung

WRITING
FROM THE
CENTER

BUCKEYE

ﻉﻠ

YEARS AFTER MY father's heart quit, I keep in a wooden box on my desk the two buckeyes that were in his pocket when he died. Once the size of plums, the brown seeds are shriveled now, hollow, hard as pebbles, yet they still gleam from the polish of his hands. He used to reach for them in his overalls or suit pants and click them together, or he would draw them out, cupped in his palm, and twirl them with his blunt carpenter's fingers, all the while humming snatches of old tunes.

"Do you really believe buckeyes keep off arthritis?" I asked him more than once.

He would flex his hands and say, "I do so far."

My father never paid much heed to pain. Near the end, when his worn knee often slipped out of joint, he would pound it back in place with a rubber mallet. If a splinter worked into his flesh beyond the reach of tweezers, he would heat the blade of his knife over a cigarette lighter and slice through the skin. He sought to ward off arthritis not because he feared pain but because he lived through his hands, and he dreaded the swelling of knuckles, the stiffening of fingers. What use would he be if he could no longer hold a hammer or guide a plow? When he was a boy he had known farmers not yet forty years old whose hands had curled into claws, men so crippled up they could not tie their own shoes, could not sign their names.

"I mean to tickle my grandchildren when they come along," he told me, "and I mean to build doll houses and turn spindles for tiny chairs on my lathe."

So he fondled those buckeyes as if they were charms, carrying them with him when our family moved from Ohio at the end of my childhood, bearing them to new homes in Louisiana, then Oklahoma, Ontario, and Mississippi, carrying them still on his final day when pain a thousand times fiercer than arthritis gripped his heart.

The box where I keep the buckeyes also comes from Ohio, made by my father from a walnut plank he bought at a farm auction. I remember the auction, remember the sagging face of the widow whose home was being sold, remember my father telling her he would prize that walnut as if he had watched the tree grow from a sapling on his own land. He did not care for pewter or silver or gold, but he cherished wood. On the rare occasions when my mother coaxed him into a museum, he ignored the paintings or porcelain and studied the exhibit cases, the banisters, the moldings, the parquet floors.

I remember him planing that walnut board, sawing it, sanding it, joining piece to piece to make foot stools, picture frames, jewelry boxes. My own box, a bit larger than a soap dish, lined with red corduroy, was meant to hold earrings and pins, not buckeyes. The top is inlaid with pieces fitted so as to bring out the grain, four diagonal joints converging from the corners toward the center. If I stare long enough at those converging lines, they float free of the box and point to a center deeper than wood.

ᘒ

I learned to recognize buckeyes and beeches, sugar maples and shagbark hickories, wild cherries, walnuts, and dozens of other trees while tramping through the Ohio woods with my father. To his eyes, their shapes, their leaves, their bark, their winter buds were as distinctive as the set of a friend's shoulders. As with friends, he was partial to some, craving their company, so he would go out of his way to visit particular trees, walking in a circle around the splayed roots of a sycamore, laying his hand against the trunk of a white oak, ruffling the feathery green boughs of a cedar.

"Trees breathe," he told me. "Listen."

I listened, and heard the stir of breath.

He was no botanist; the names and uses he taught me were those he had learned from country folks, not from books. Latin never crossed his lips. Only much later would I discover that the tree he called ironwood, its branches like muscular arms, good for axe handles, is known in the books as hophornbeam; what he called tuliptree or canoewood, ideal for log cabins, is officially the yellow poplar; what he called hoop ash, good for barrels and fence posts, appears in books as hackberry.

When he introduced me to the buckeye, he broke off a chunk of the gray bark and held it to my nose. I gagged.

"That's why the old-timers called it stinking buckeye," he told me. "They used it for cradles and feed troughs and peg legs."

"Why for peg legs?" I asked.

"Because it's light and hard to split, so it won't shatter when you're clumping around."

He showed me this tree in late summer, when the fruits had fallen and the ground was littered with prickly brown pods. He picked up one, as fat as a lemon, and peeled away the husk to reveal the shiny seed. He laid it in my palm and closed my fist around it so the seed peeped out from the circle formed by my index finger and thumb. "You see where it got the name?" he asked.

I saw: what gleamed in my hand was the eye of a deer, bright with life. "It's beautiful," I said.

"It's beautiful," my father agreed, "but also poisonous. Nobody eats buckeyes, except maybe a fool squirrel."

I knew the gaze of deer from living in the Ravenna Arsenal, in Portage County, up in the northeastern corner of Ohio. After supper we often drove the Arsenal's gravel roads, past the munitions bunkers, past acres of rusting tanks and wrecked bombers, into the far fields where we counted deer. One June evening, while mist rose from the ponds, we counted three hundred and eleven, our family record. We found the deer in herds, in bunches, in amorous pairs. We came upon lone bucks, their antlers lifted against the sky like the bare branches of dogwood. If you were quiet, if your hands were empty, if you moved slowly, you could leave the car and steal to within a few paces of a grazing deer, close enough to see the delicate lips, the twitching nostrils, the glossy, fathomless eyes.

ᘒ

The wooden box on my desk holds these grazing deer, as it holds the buckeyes and the walnut plank and the farm auction and the munitions bunkers and the breathing forests and my father's hands. I could lose the box, I could lose the polished seeds, but if I were to lose the memories I would become a bush without roots, and every new breeze would toss me about. All those memories lead back to the northeastern corner of Ohio, the place where I came to consciousness, where I learned to connect feelings with words, where I fell in love with the earth.

It was a troubled love, for much of the land I knew as a child had been ravaged. The ponds in the Arsenal teemed with bluegill and beaver, but they were also laced with TNT from the making of bombs. Because the wolves and coyotes had long since been killed, some of the deer, so plump in the June grass, collapsed on the January snow, whittled by hunger to racks of bones. Outside the Arsenal's high barbed fences, many of the farms had failed, their barns caving in, their topsoil gone. Ravines were choked with swollen couches and junked washing machines and cars. Crossing fields, you had to be careful not to slice your feet on tin cans or shards of glass. Most of the rivers had been dammed, turning fertile valleys into scummy playgrounds for boats.

One free-flowing river, the Mahoning, ran past the small farm near the Arsenal where our family lived during my later years in Ohio. We owned just enough land to pasture three ponies and to grow vegetables for our table, but those few acres opened onto miles of woods and creeks and secret meadows. I walked that land in every season, every weather, following animal trails. But then the Mahoning, too, was doomed by a government decision; we were forced to sell our land, and a dam began to rise across the river.

If enough people had spoken for the river, we might have saved it. If enough people had believed that our scarred country was worth defending, we might have dug in our heels and fought. Our attachments to the land were all private. We had no shared lore, no literature, no art to root us there, to give us courage, to help us stand our ground. The only maps we had were those issued by the state, showing a maze of numbered lines stretched over emptiness. The Ohio landscape never showed up on postcards or posters, never unfurled like tapestry in films, rarely filled even a paragraph in books. There were no mountains in that place, no waterfalls, no rocky gorges, no vistas. It was a country of low hills, cut over woods, scoured fields, villages that had lost their purpose, roads that had lost their way.

"Let us love the country of here below," Simone Weil urged. "It is real; it offers resistance to love. It is this country that God has given us to love. He has willed that it should be difficult yet possible to love it." Which is the deeper truth about buckeyes,

[5]

their poison or their beauty? I hold with the beauty; or rather, I am held by the beauty, without forgetting the poison. In my corner of Ohio the gullies were choked with trash, yet cedars flickered up like green flames from cracks in stone; in the evening bombs exploded at the ammunition dump, yet from the darkness came the mating cries of owls. I was saved from despair by knowing a few men and women who cared enough about the land to clean up trash, who planted walnuts and oaks that would long outlive them, who imagined a world that would have no call for bombs.

How could our hearts be large enough for heaven if they are not large enough for earth? The only country I am certain of is the one here below. The only paradise I know is the one lit by our everyday sun, this land of difficult love, shot through with shadow. The place where we learn this love, if we learn it at all, shimmers behind every new place we inhabit.

ₛₐ

A family move carried me away from Ohio thirty years ago; my schooling and marriage and job have kept me away ever since, except for visits in memory and in flesh. I returned to the site of our farm one cold November day, when the trees were skeletons and the ground shone with the yellow of fallen leaves. From a previous trip I knew that our house had been bulldozed, our yard and pasture had grown up in thickets, and the reservoir had flooded the woods. On my earlier visit I had merely gazed from the car, too numb with loss to climb out. But on this November day, I parked the car, drew on my hat and gloves, opened the door, and walked.

I was looking for some sign that we had lived there, some token of our affection for the place. All that I recognized, aside from the contours of the land, were two weeping willows that my father and I had planted near the road. They had been slips the length of my forearm when we set them out, and now their crowns rose higher than the telephone poles. When I touched them last, their trunks had been smooth and supple, as thin as my wrist, and now they were furrowed and stout. I took off my gloves and laid my hands against the rough bark. Immediately I felt the wince of tears. Without knowing why, I said hello to my father, quietly at first, then louder and louder, as if only shouts could reach him through the bark and miles and years.

Surprised by sobs, I turned from the willows and stumbled away toward the drowned woods, calling to my father. I sensed that he was nearby. Even as I called, I was wary of grief's deceptions. I had never seen his body after he died. By the time I reached the place of his death, a furnace had reduced him to ashes. The need to see him, to let go of him, to let go of this land and time, was powerful enough to summon mirages; I knew that. But I also knew, stumbling toward the woods, that my father was here.

At the bottom of a slope where the creek used to run, I came to an expanse of gray stumps and withered grass. It was a bay of the reservoir from which the water had retreated, the level drawn down by engineers or drought. I stood at the edge of this desolate ground, willing it back to life, trying to recall the woods where my father had taught me the names of trees. No green shoots rose. I walked out among the stumps. The grass crackled under my boots, breath rasped in my throat, but otherwise the world was silent.

Then a cry broke overhead and I looked up to see a red-tailed hawk launching out from the top of an oak. I recognized the bird from its band of dark feathers across the creamy breast and the tail splayed like rosy fingers against the sun. It was a red-tailed hawk for sure; and it was also my father. Not a symbol of my father, not a reminder, not a ghost, but the man himself, right there, circling in the air above me. I knew this as clearly as I knew the sun burned in the sky. A calm poured through me. My chest quit heaving. My eyes dried.

Hawk and father wheeled above me, circle upon circle, wings

barely moving, head still. My own head was still, looking up, knowing and being known. Time scattered like fog. At length, father and hawk stroked the air with those powerful wings, three beats, then vanished over a ridge.

The voice of my education told me then and tells me now that I did not meet my father, that I merely projected my longing onto a bird. My education may well be right; yet nothing I heard in school, nothing I've read, no lesson reached by logic has ever convinced me as utterly or stirred me as deeply as did that red-tailed hawk. Nothing in my education prepared me to love a piece of the earth, least of all a humble, battered country like northeastern Ohio; I learned from the land itself.

Before leaving the drowned woods, I looked around at the ashen stumps, the wilted grass, and for the first time since moving from this place I was able to let it go. This ground was lost; the flood would reclaim it. But other ground could be saved, must be saved, in every watershed, every neighborhood. For each home ground we need new maps, living maps, stories and poems, photographs and paintings, essays and songs. We need to know where we are, so that we may dwell in our place with a full heart.

BENEATH THE SMOOTH
SKIN OF AMERICA

રેે

I BEGAN LIFE by supposing, as all children do, that my home ground was the world. Nothing existed apart from what I could touch and sniff and see. The sun rose from our woods, crossed our sky, set beyond the barbed wire fence of our pasture, and shone nowhere else. The telephone poles along the road out front of our house dwindled away to nothingness at the edge of my vision. Cars passed along that road, swelling and shrinking, aimless as clouds, and the road itself led only to our door. Neighbors often appeared on our porch, and strangers sometimes, but where they came from I could not imagine. In my earliest conscious days, I never suspected that the world rolled on beyond the reach of my senses.

Only by leaving that familiar ground did I discover that it was merely one place among many places. In addition to our house and barn and the surrounding fields, I soon realized, there were other houses on other roads, and there was a white church with brown carpet that smelled of mold, and a glassy store where bananas grinned at me as I trundled by in a silver cart. At the end of an automobile ride, there was a whole town crowded with stores, and a stone building filled with books on shelves, and a garage ripe with oil, and a welding shop bright with sparks, and a cinema where giant pictures danced on the wall. Beyond that nearby town, I discovered, there were other towns, such as Warren, where candy lifesavers came from, and there were cities like Akron, where the blimp lived and the air stank of rubber, and Cleveland, where the lake was too wide to see across. With every journey I took, the world seemed larger and more various.

On trips from that childhood place in Ohio to my father's native Mississippi, I knew I had left familiar territory when the accents in roadside cafes began to slow and thicken, when grits and black-eyed peas showed up on menus, when signs appeared on gas station toilets marked "Colored" or "White," and corn in the fields gave way to cotton or tobacco, and the soil turned from brown to red, and the sun hammered down on the roof of our car like a fist. Traveling in July or August, we drove south into a scorched country where the dust burned my nose and the water surprised my tongue and the trees shook with a strange light.

The watermelons and peanuts my father planted each spring in our Great Lakes garden hardly ever bore, but down in Mississippi on my grandparents' farm we helped dig peanuts by the bushel, and the melons were so abundant, we could eat the heart and leave the rest. Birds woke me there at dawn with songs I had never heard in Ohio. Even the crowing of roosters and barking of dogs and buzzing of insects sounded foreign. Why, even I sounded foreign, down there in Mississippi. My southern cousins begged me to talk Yankee for them. What did they want me to say? Anything at all, so long as it was pure Yankee. I babbled obligingly, aware in their company that I, too, had an accent, that I bore the imprint of my home ground.

From those Mississippi kinfolk, I learned to think of myself as a Northerner. I never thought of myself as a Midwesterner until I left Ohio for college in Rhode Island. The people I met there, who came mostly from cities bordering the Atlantic or Pacific, claimed they could hear the rustle of cornstalks in my voice, could see the roll of glacial plains in my walk, could detect in my manners and politics the domes of county courthouses and the steeples of country churches. I doubt that my origins showed quite so plainly; but my fellow students, on hearing where I was from, saw what they expected to see.

Who else but a Midwesterner, they asked me, would refuse to drink alcohol, smoke dope, or sleep with a willing girl, refuse even to swear? I was considered a bit odd back home as well, I answered; but they were not listening. Where else but in the Midwest, they wanted to know, could one find the garish, baggy shirts I wore? My mother had sewn those shirts, I answered. There, you see, who else but a Midwesterner would wear shirts his mother had made? I was as square, my new friends assured me, as the wheat fields they had spied from airplanes while zooming over the vast, vague, lonesome land that separated the Allegheny Mountains from the Rockies.

ॐ

I started college and made the last of those family trips to Mississippi in the year John Kennedy was killed. Now, three decades later, would a teenager moving from rural Ohio to Rhode Island be so easily identified as a Midwesterner? Would a child traveling south from the neighborhood of Lake Erie pass through zones of greater and greater strangeness, finally arriving in Mississippi as though in a foreign country, to be greeted there as an unmistakable Yankee?

It would depend on the teenager and the child, of course, and on how widely they had traveled, and on their destination. But even a homebody, packed off to kinfolk or to college half a continent away, would not experience today the vivid regional differences that were common thirty and forty years ago, because many of those differences have been erased.

Suppose you take a young traveler from a suburb, perhaps the third or fourth suburb of the child's life, the sort of place where the layout of roads and landscaping of lawns and floor plans of houses and even the food in the refrigerator and the furniture in the living room have become standard issue, coast to coast. With child buckled in, car windows shut, you slide a tape into the deck, turn on the air conditioner, pull onto the interstate, and cruise, pausing only to gas up at filling stations or to eat at fastfood mills, the same brands beckoning from every cloverleaf with unvarying architecture and colors and wares. The herds of houses and shopping strips you can see from the highway look pretty much like the ones your child already knows. The trees have been cut back from the pavement to a safe distance, baring the roadsides to litter and grass. Now and again you might be able to glimpse farm fields, but as you tear past at a mile a minute you would be hard put to name what is growing or grazing there. You would also be hard put to name the rivers you hurtle across on bridges, the hills that suddenly rise and sink, the valleys that yawn and vanish, or the inconvenient mountains. If you stop to gaze at natural wonders—the Grand Canyon, say, or the Everglades—chances are they will look messier and duller than they do in movies, even assuming you can maneuver through traffic and shoulder through crowds for a clear view.

At night on this journey you sleep in your favorite chain of motels, where you know the color of the bedspread and the design of the wallpaper before opening the door, and where you watch on cable television your customary shows. Arriving by and by at your destination—perhaps in another suburb where your sister's family now lives, also their third or fourth address, or in a condominium where your parents have briefly settled—you may only be able to prove that you have traveled at all by checking the odometer on the car. Chances are the local mall will feature the same stores, the same products, the same movies, and, so far as you can tell from a quick visit, the same customers as the mall back home. In what sense have you in fact left home? Could you have simply driven to the far side of your own town and seen as much novelty? With every such journey a child takes—from the familiar to the familiar by way of the familiar—the smaller and more homogeneous the world seems.

≈

Of course I exaggerate. But by how much? America is still a manifold and textured land, nor could any human force ever wear it down to utter uniformity; but each year it is rubbed a bit smoother by technology and commerce, by the media, and by our feverish mobility. The more we gad about, chasing dollars and dreams, the less of an imprint we bear from any particular place, and the less likely we are to know in depth the place where we happen to be. Local accents give way before the monotone of television. Local foods give way to packaged fare. Local methods of building or courting, local songs and stories and ideas give way to nationwide models. Consider what it means for a lone purchasing agent to choose the novels that will be sold in a chain of bookstores stretching from Connecticut to California, for identical prefab houses to roll into Louisiana bayous and Montana mountains, for the shoes endorsed by a star athlete to adorn ten million teenage feet, or for the images of a single advertising campaign to glimmer in a hundred million heads.

A few years ago, Holiday Inn ran a series of ads under the slogan, "No Surprises." Nothing unpleasant would befall you in any of their hundreds of motels, they promised, for you would know beforehand precisely what to expect. And what roadweary traveler has not felt the allure of the familiar? Any chain of stores, any brand of goods, any broadcast network might well embrace that slogan, because they flourish by appealing to our yen for the predictable. It's an old yearning. All empires, from ancient Rome to modern McDonald's, seek to impose a uniform scheme on as much of the world as they can master. Our own young nation spread one surveying grid over the whole continent west of the Ohio River, the same for deserts and rainforests, mountains and swamps. The vendors of elevator music dissolve bluegrass banjos and Cajun accordions and jazz trombones into one bland prattle, and the makers of TV dinners reduce the world's cuisines to indistinguishable pap. From slicing out identical squares of real estate to stamping out identical parts in factories to dishing out identical meals in franchises, we have been following the slope of our desire for the safely known.

The trouble is, we cannot banish ugly surprises without banishing lovely ones as well. The unexpected may annoy us, but may also wake us up. If you seal your windows against the odor of skunks and the shriek of sirens, you will also miss the lilacs and finches, the yeasty breath of bakeries and the playground squeal of children. If you cross the country and order the routine burger and fries without needing to look at the menu, chances are you will not taste what you eat. If you have been greeted in a dozen states by clerks wearing the same hairdo and smile, if you have heard everywhere the same remarks from talk show hosts, have seen on every newsstand the same reports of blood and lust, your brain may well shut down for lack of anything to do. We have good evolutionary reason to fear the unknown, for it may poison us, bewilder us, or devour us. But we have equally good reason to crave the unknown, for it may feed, renew, or enlighten us. We learn by coming up against what we do not already know.

In the long run, evolution favors curiosity and diversity—which is why we travel and why all empires eventually break down. In the short run, however, barring a catastrophe, no force of nature or culture seems likely to halt the homogenizing of America. Since I refuse to root for catastrophe, I find myself considering how we might redraw the map of our country as the old regional distinctions fade away. If we still need to be able to say where we are from, as I believe we do, how might we define a new sense of home territory? As the human veneer we have laid over the continent becomes ever smoother, what new landmarks do we reckon by?

ॐ

Clearly, we are well rid of some old regional markers, such as those "Colored" and "White" signs over toilets, or the statues of black jockeys faithfully holding lanterns beside front doors, or cigar store Indians; and we are well rid of the accompanying bigotry, booster-ism, and smarm. We could get along fine without the phony regionalism symbolized by Confederate flags, by squinty-eyed cowboys peddling cigarettes from billboards, by posters of farm couples bearing pitchforks and grimaces, by hillbilly shows and blackface minstrels, by souvenir shoppes crammed with gen-u-ine trinkets that have been mass-produced in Third World sweat-shops, by the prettified images of travel brochures. Better to leave the map of our country blank than to smear it with lies.

The blurring of regional boundaries may be liberating, if it makes us less eager to judge one another in light of birthplaces or mailing addresses. Although I have lived most of my life in areas where hayseeds, rednecks, and Bible-thumpers are supposed to breed, I have yet to meet a person who could be adequately summed up by any of those epithets. A generation after I left Ohio for college in Rhode Island, my daughter has left Indiana for the same place, and I would be delighted if she never has to wear the old Midwestern identity like an ill-fitting, moth-eaten, hand-me-down suit.

Instead of patching up old regional costumes, therefore, we ought to clothe ourselves with a new sense of place. How? Many voices now urge us to let go of our local attachments, forego geography, and move into the global village constructed by the media and the multinational corporations. That is a cozy metaphor—the global village—but a false one. In a real village, you are answerable to your neighbors, you are bound by love as well as duty to care for nearby streets and fields, you are known by your acts. In the global village we are only passersby, without power or responsibility, free to come or go, tune in or out. We may at times be moved to dial 800-numbers, write checks, or vote, yet even the most compassionate of viewers, fed on a diet of disaster, will eventually grow numb.

Other voices, here and abroad, run to the opposite extreme from the global visionaries and advocate a sort of ethnic regionalism, a sense of belonging defined by race, religion, or national origins rather than geography. Blood is thicker than dirt, so the argument goes. I will leave that path to others, because I am one of those mongrels unable to claim membership in any ethnic group. Besides, I notice how often a path that starts from blood ends with bloodshed.

Still other voices urge us to recover a sense of region by scouting the back alleys and back roads, where vestiges of local culture still survive. I have scouted my share, for I am drawn to out-of-the-way spots and stubborn characters. I am fascinated by artifacts and turns of speech and ways of living that have endured because they embody a wisdom worked out in relation to place. Yet I have grown wary of culture-collecting, which too often becomes a search for the merely quaint—a handmade quilt to hang on the wall, a quirky phrase to slip into conversation, a split-oak basket to hold the deli bread. Just as fashion designers offer a peasant look without the nuisance of a peasant life, so the slick regional magazines offer page after page of local color, picturesque scenes for us to contemplate but not to inhabit.

The earth needs fewer tourists and more inhabitants, it seems to me—fewer people who float about in bubbles of money and more people committed to knowing and tending their home ground. So I suggest we begin our search for a new sense of place not by tuning in to the global village, nor by tracing our ancestry, nor by studying our own remarkable works, but by learning all we can about the land. What soils surround our houses or apartments and what rocks underlie them? How did those soils and bedrocks form, how have they been wrenched and rumpled by the sliding of the earth's plates, how have they been shaped by the long strokes of weather, perhaps by glaciers or volcanoes, and how do they hold and channel water? As for water, we need to know how much of it falls each year in the neighborhood, and where the rain goes after it slides off the roof, into what sewers or creeks, what aquifers, what rivers and lakes, what bay, what sea. Where does the sun rise and set throughout the year, how does the light change, and how do the shadows play? We should observe the seasonal drama of the air, its heat and cold, its moisture and color, its fragrances. We need to know which way the winds blow, and what dust or pollen or pollution they carry. What birds, beasts, insects, and wild plants are native to the area? What crops thrive there? What bushes and flowers and trees blossom in that place, and when? What creatures sing?

The answers to such questions help reveal where we actually live. They point to durable realities that have shaped human existence for millions of years, and that will continue to shape our existence so long as we dwell on this planet. Biologists refer to those durable realities by terms such as watershed, biome, habitat, food-chain, climate, topography, ecosystem, and the areas defined by these natural features they call bioregions. Knowing those terms and what they stand for will be of far more use to us in understanding our place, than will knowing the outlines of townships and counties and states, those airy abstractions. It is handy to parcel the land into governmental districts named Chicago, say, or Illinois, or the United States of America; but the earth ignores our tidy partitions.

Beneath the smooth human surface, behind the maps, beyond all our blasting and bulldozing, the land itself remains extraordinarily diverse. To say that pine forests in Maine and chemlawn subdivisions in Connecticut belong to New England, or that Washington's Olympic Peninsula and the Texas panhandle belong to the West, or that Kentucky strip mines and Carolina cypress swamps belong to the South, or that the stony lakes of upstate Minnesota and the tallgrass prairies of Kansas and the limestone hills of southern Indiana all belong to the Midwest, is not to say very much. The old regional labels have been stretched so thin as to become transparent.

We need a richer vocabulary of place. On average, according to geographers, there are fewer place names per square mile in the United States than anywhere else on earth. In long-settled countries such as Ireland, and in the few portions of our own country where memory has been sustained over centuries—as in the Hopi mesas and the Mohawk Valley of the Iroquois—every watercourse, every bluff or butte, every prominent rock bears a name and a story. In the same way, we need to be able to speak about the particulars, the subtleties, the varieties of all our places.

We cannot help but carry the land in our bodies, for that is the only source of our bodies; we must make a deliberate effort, however, if we are to carry the land in our minds. Bioregions are not easily named or neatly circumscribed, for natural boundaries overlap, watersheds cut across climate zones, species shift their range, habitats change. Still, if we pay attention, we begin to notice patterns in the local landscape. Perceiving those patterns, acquiring names and theories and stories for them, we cease to be tourists and become inhabitants. The bioregional consciousness I am talking about means bearing your place in mind, keeping track of its condition and needs, committing yourself to its care.

❧

Taking part in the small-scale rediscovery of your home region does not prevent you from also taking part in the large-scale reimagining of our common home and common fate on earth, an awakening that René Dubos has called the planetization of consciousness. Every thread you discover in the local web of life leads beyond your place to life elsewhere.

The limestone beneath the foundations of my house here in Indiana was formed in a great inland sea that stretched from what is now Pennsylvania across the Great Plains. The honeysuckle that blooms in my backyard is a wild offspring of plants brought to this country from Asia. The swifts that nest in my chimney spend their winters in the Amazon basin. And the mulberry, one of our neighborhood trees, flourishes from Massachusetts to Florida, from Minnesota to Oklahoma.

I am writing these pages in June, the season hereabouts when mulberries come ripe and chimney swifts lace the sky with chatter and honeysuckle sweetens the air. On my walks lately I have been pausing at mulberry trees to munch the fruit, dark purple berries the size of thimbles. One day I was grazing on a tree close to the park, as blissful as any bear among blueberries, my lips and fingers stained the color of beets, when a man I know came walking by with his two young daughters.

The girls stopped to gawk at me, and the older of them said, "You're eating off a tree."

"I sure am," I answered between mouthfuls.

"What're you eating?" the girl asked.

"Mulberries." I held out a palmful of the plump fruits. "They're delicious. Maybe your dad will let you try some."

The girls looked hopefully at their father, who seized each of them by the hand and led them away, declaring, "Thank you very much, but we never eat anything that grows wild. Never ever."

If you hold by that rule, you will not get sick from eating poison berries, but neither will you be nourished from eating sweet

[19]

ones. Why not learn to distinguish the one from the other? Why feed belly and mind only from packages? Children who can identify a brand of sneakers from fifty yards away can learn to identify trees and bushes, flowers and mushrooms. Any child or adult who can recognize a pop tune from the opening three notes can learn to recognize the songs of neighborhood birds. Anyone who can recite dialogue from a hit movie or follow the plot of a soap opera should be able to grasp the natural history of a bioregion.

Most of our children spend a year in grade school studying the history of their home state. Shouldn't they spend at least as much time studying their home ground? Let them take walks, handle stones and leaves and dirt, watch squirrels and bats and bugs, pore over photographs and fossils and maps, feel the land in their bones. We grown-ups could explore along with them. You don't need a degree in biology to listen for geese honking by overhead, to see burst milkweed pods loose their downy seeds, to run your fingers over the ledges in roadcuts, to watch a storm blow in from the horizon, to sample water from a creek, to discover any of the countless details that make up the life of a place.

What humans do is certainly part of the life of a place. In most areas, in fact, our doings are so conspicuous that we may mistake them for the whole show, when they are only minor acts. That is why, in reimagining one's region, it is safer to begin by studying the land than by studying the yellow pages. Informed by a sense of natural history, we should be ready to learn the human history, the tales that have been told, the songs that have been sung; we should be able to see more clearly how the land has invited certain kinds of work and worship and community, and how in turn our presence has transformed the land. Alert to the slow rhythms of nature, we can appraise more soberly the hectic rhythms of the headlines.

If we are to live responsibly on earth, we will have to recognize that our true address is not the one listed in the phone book, but the one defined by the movement of water, the lay of the land, the dirt and air, the animals and plants, as well as by the patterns of human occupation, the buildings and crops, the language and lore. To discover our true address, we will have to stay off the interstates, avoid the friendly franchises, climb out of our cars, hunt up guides who have lived heedfully in place, and we will have to walk around with eyes and ears open to the neighborhood. Knowledge in depth about one's home region will not strip away the gleaming surface that has been spread over the continent by mass culture and mass production, but such knowledge may reveal to us how thin that surface is, thin enough to see through, as thin as ice on a spring pond.

IMAGINING THE MIDWEST

ॐ

EVEN BEFORE THE last shots of the Revolution had been fired, settlers began crossing the Allegheny Mountains into the wild interior of America. They traveled on foot, on horseback, in jouncing wagons, cautiously, unsure of their destinations. In leaky boats they paddled or drifted along the great rivers—Ohio, Mississippi, Missouri—and the many lesser ones, bearing axes and rifles and Bibles, clocks and spinning wheels and churns. They carried far more baggage in their heads than in their hands: notions of God, recipes, remedies, designs for barns and quilts, rules of right and wrong, knowledge of blacksmithing or weaving, old languages from Europe spiced with American lingo, fears and hopes, stories and songs. They were looking for elbow room, freedom, a fresh start, but above all they were looking for land.

The land they found beyond the Ohio River was generally flat or rolling, fertile, wet, dark with forest in the east, bounded by lakes in the north and by hills or feverish swamps in the south, giving way farther west to seas of grass. No soil back in the old colonies was so good for corn, wheat, oats, or beans; no woods elsewhere could fatten hogs so quickly; no place in the world, as far as the settlers knew, could rival the bounty of this ground. The newcomers would not understand for a generation or two the role that oceans and glaciers had played in shaping the terrain, nor would they understand how the soil's fertility depended on steady rainfall and the slow seethe of plants.

That rich territory had been inhabited already for thousands of years, by people who left behind earthworks, pots, carved shells, chipped stones, and more recently by people whose alien names sounded to the settlers like Shawnee, Miami, Wyandot, Ojibwa, Potawatomi, Winnebago, Kickapoo, Lakota. In little more than a century following the Revolution, all but a remnant of these native tribes were killed off or cleared out, all the desirable land was claimed, and the region was carved up into twelve states. Ohio came first, admitted to the Union in 1803; South and North Dakota were the latest to join, in 1889; and in between came Indiana, Illinois, and Iowa, Michigan and Missouri, Wisconsin and Minnesota, Kansas and Nebraska.

For all that vast interior the early settlers had no certain name. They spoke of it as the wilderness, the frontier, the Promised Land, the Territory Northwest of the Ohio River, or simply as the West. Walt Whitman called it "this continental inland West." Mark Twain called it "the body of the nation." Only in the last decade of the nineteenth century, when the frontier had long since moved on beyond the prairies, beyond the high plains and the Rocky Mountains to the shore of the Pacific, did the twelve-state region come to be known as the Middle West. Tongues soon wore that phrase down to the twin syllables of "Midwest." Writers in our own century, hunting as always for metaphors that will stick in the mind, have called it the Midlands, the Middle Border, the Corn Belt, the Breadbasket, the Inland Sea, the Great Valley, the Heartland, the Heart of the Country.

Whatever the name, this is my home region. Reared in Ohio, seasoned in Indiana, well traveled from the Great Lakes to the tallgrass prairies, from the Ozarks to the Boundary Waters, I am a

Midwesterner through and through. In Fairbanks, Alaska; in San Francisco, Santa Fe, and New Orleans; in Boston and Washington and places even farther flung, I have met folks who listened to my speech and squinted at my gestures and gauged my opinions before asking me, "You're from the Midwest, aren't you?" I accept the label without knowing clearly what it means, about myself or my place. Are there Midwestern traits of culture or character? Is there a distinctive Midwestern landscape, inner or outer? Because regional terms refer to states of mind as much as they do to geography, and because I am a writer, I have been looking in literature for some understanding of the immense and elusive territory looming behind all the labels.

ॐ

The Heartland began producing corn and hogs, schools and rapscallions right away, but it only began producing literature of note after the Civil War, timidly with Edward Eggleston's *The Hoosier School-Master* in 1871, boldly with Mark Twain's Mississippi Valley books in the following decade. Reckoning from the publication of *Adventures of Huckleberry Finn* in 1885, we have had just over a century's worth of serious writing about the Midwest, most of it composed from a distance by men and women who grew up in the region and who then moved to places more stimulating, more fashionable, or more hospitable to art.

Eggleston recollected Indiana from New York, as Samuel Clemens recollected life on the Mississippi from his mansion in Connecticut. Hemingway recalled Michigan from the clarifying distance of Paris. Willa Cather and Wright Morris wrote about Nebraska from opposite coasts, Cather on the Atlantic, Morris on the Pacific. William Stafford kept making poems about Kansas while living in Oregon. The pattern continues today, for Toni Morrison writes about Ohio from New Jersey, Louise Erdrich writes about North Dakota from New Hampshire, and W. P. Kinsella writes about Iowa from various spots in Canada. Unlike the great literature of New England or the South—composed by stay-at-homes such as Thoreau and Hawthorne and Frost, by Faulkner and O'Connor and Welty—the notable literature of the Midwest is largely absentee.

Why this pattern of exile among our best writers? It is too easy to say that writers always migrate to publishing centers, where dollars and reputations are to be made. True, William Dean Howells could not have edited the *Atlantic Monthly* from his childhood towns in Ohio. T. S. Eliot could not have rubbed shoulders with Ezra Pound back home in St. Louis. Yet Faulkner was never published and not much read in Oxford, Mississippi, nor was O'Connor in Milledgeville, Georgia, nor was Thoreau in Concord, Massachusetts; and all three stayed on their home ground. Midwestern writers have not been so much lured elsewhere, I suspect, as driven out, by a combination of puritanical religion, utilitarian economics, and anti-intellectualism.

The Middle West was the first region of the United States to be settled after the definitive break from the Old World, the first to bear the stamp of the raw, rambunctious democracy. When the Frenchman Alexis de Tocqueville toured the United States in the early 1830s, just as a new society was forming in the wild interior, he remarked that "The religion professed by the first emigrants, and bequeathed by them to their descendants,—simple in its forms, austere and almost harsh in its principles, and hostile to external symbols and to ceremonial pomp,—is naturally unfavorable to the fine arts, and only yields reluctantly to the pleasures of literature." Nowhere was that religion harsher, fiercer, more hostile to sensuality or speculation than in the Midwest—or at least so it has seemed to our writers.

Tocqueville also observed in the new republic a stifling complacency: "No writer, whatever be his eminence, can escape paying this tribute of adulation to his fellow-citizens. The majority lives in the perpetual utterance of self-applause." According to reports from travelers, this charge was especially true for the brash young region out beyond the Ohio. On the Prairie Home Companion radio show in the 1990s, you can still hear an ironic, muted echo of that view in Garrison Keillor's description of Lake Wobegon, Minnesota, as a place where all the men are strong, all the women are good-looking, and all the children are above average.

When Charles Dickens published an account of his own American tour, including an arduous circuit through the Ohio Valley, he outraged his readers in the United States by mixing disgruntled criticism with praise. How dare he complain that the citizens of the freest country on earth had manners as filthy as the hogs that ran in their stump-filled streets? How dare he regard their democracy as a form of mob rule? How could he possibly describe the Ohio woods as tedious, the Illinois prairie as dull, the mighty Mississippi as a hideous ditch? So angry was the reception of his *American Notes* (1842) that Dickens was still trying to soothe the frazzled nerves of audiences on his return visit to the United States a quarter century later.

He might have been forewarned of this reaction by reading Tocqueville, who explained that "If America has not as yet had any great writers, the reason is given in these facts; there can be no literary genius without freedom of opinion, and freedom of opinion does not exist in America." That judgment was too hard on the country as a whole: at the time of the Frenchman's tour, Jefferson had only recently died, Lincoln was preparing to give up soldiering for politics, Cooper and Irving were still active, and Emerson, Hawthorne, and Poe were showing the first glints of their genius; according to the testimony of Midwestern writers, however, it was a fair enough judgment on the Heartland, not only in the 1830s but right up to our own day.

In *Main-Travelled Roads* (1891), Hamlin Garland described an upper Midwest inhabited by "Puritan families" who led joyless, toilsome lives in dreary houses: "There were no books, no music, and only a few newspapers in sight—a bare, blank, cold, drab-colored shelter from the rain, not a home. Nothing cosey, nothing heart-warming; a grim and horrible shed." A generation later, in *Spoon River Anthology* (1915), Edgar Lee Masters chronicled the desolation of spirit, the crushing of free thought and fine feeling in an Illinois town. Even those few sensitive souls who managed to run away could not shake off the smothering influence of their origins, as the painter Archibald Higbie discovered in far-off Rome:

> There was no culture, you know, in Spoon River,
> And I burned with shame and held my peace.
> And what could I do, all covered over
> And weighted down with western soil,
> Except aspire, and pray for another
> Birth in the world, with all of Spoon River
> Rooted out of my soul?

Whether or not they uproot themselves, citizens of the literary Midwest commonly burn with shame. In Winesburg, a composite of the small towns that Sherwood Anderson knew while growing up in Ohio, one character after another is driven to misery or despair by the judgment of neighbors. Almost every story in *Winesburg, Ohio* (1919) presents a suffering figure whose private ways come in conflict with the town's rigid rules. Those who break the rules may be ridiculed or shunned, may even be threatened with hanging. Anderson himself was vilified, as he saw it, for admitting that "sex had something to do with people's lives." His readers were shocked, above all in Ohio: "No one it seemed ever used a profane word. And bringing sex back to take what seemed to us its normal place in the picture of life, we were called sex-obsessed."

[27]

When I was growing up in Anderson's home state, more than forty years after publication of *Winesburg, Ohio*, the book was still frequently banned from schools and pulled from libraries, for suggesting—as I once heard an indignant parent say—that "God is a big question mark and man is just an animal." The copy I read, secretly, at age thirteen or fourteen was borrowed from a boy who had moved to our neighborhood from Connecticut, and who was known to be racy because he smoked cigars. I could not help but identify with George Willard, the young reporter who gathers the town's dark stories and who dreams through the whole book of escaping from Winesburg to "some city," where life will be larger. Willard's own mother has been a victim of gossip, and her life, without room to unfold, has been twisted and cramped. In his itch to move on—an itch that culminates in a final story called "Departure"—George Willard sums up the restlessness of his creator and of sundry Midwestern characters, both fictional and real, including my own teenage self.

Although Willa Cather found much to prize about the land she had left, in *O Pioneers!* (1913) and *My Ántonia* (1918) she also lamented the backwardness of rural Nebraska, and she made sure that all of her aspiring artists and intellectuals moved away to the cities. Jim Burden, the narrator of *My Ántonia*, winds up as a lawyer in New York. Describing his Nebraska town of Black Hawk, he might be speaking for any of dozens of heroes or heroines in Midwestern literature who flee from their home places:

> On starlight nights I used to pace up and down those long, cold streets, scowling at the little, sleeping houses on either side, with their storm-windows and covered back porches. They were flimsy shelters, most of them poorly built of light wood, with spindle porch-posts horribly mutilated by the turning-lathe. Yet for all their frailness, how much jealousy and envy and unhappiness some of them managed to contain! The life that went on in them seemed to me made up of evasions and negations; shifts to save cooking, to save washing and cleaning,

devices to propitiate the tongue of gossip. This guarded mode of existence was like living under a tyranny. People's speech, their voices, their very glances, became furtive and repressed. Every individual taste, every natural appetite, was bridled by caution.

Caution, repression, tyranny, the desire for respectability and the bridling of appetite: those hindering qualities turn up repeatedly in portrayals of the Midwest, from *Huckleberry Finn* to Toni Morrison's *Beloved* (1987).

Sinclair Lewis won fame and fortune by attacking Midwestern towns for their materialism and smugness and conformity. The name of his title character in *Babbitt* (1922) has entered our language as the label for a person who cares only about money and appearances and nothing at all about the life of the mind. Carol Kennicott, the heroine of *Main Street* (1920), battles vainly against the "village nothingness" of Gopher Prairie, Minnesota, where she feels oppressed by "an unimaginatively standardized background, a sluggishness of speech and manners, a rigid ruling of the spirit by the desire to be respectable." Her neighbors strike her as "savorless people, gulping tasteless food, and sitting afterward, coatless and thoughtless, in rocking-chairs prickly with inane decorations, listening to mechanical music, saying mechanical things about the excellence of Ford automobiles, and viewing themselves as the greatest race in the world." Everywhere she turns, she feels "the demand for standardized behavior coming in waves from all the citizens who sat in their sitting-rooms watching her with respectable eyes, waiting, demanding, unyielding." Little wonder, a suffragette from Washington explains to Carol, for the "'Middlewest is double-Puritan—prairie Puritan on top of New England Puritan; bluff frontiersman on the surface, but in its heart it still has the ideal of Plymouth Rock in a sleet-storm.'"

ª

The discouraging words of those earlier Midwestern books weighed on me as my wife and I were deciding, after graduate school, whether to accept a job that would oblige us to move from England to Indiana. Were the judgments of more recent books still so bleak? When I came upon a new collection of stories by an author who was living in northern Indiana, I read it eagerly; but I found few encouraging words in Williams Gass's *In the Heart of the Heart of the Country* (1968). At one point in the title story, the narrator quotes the withering appraisal of a nineteenth-century visitor to the Hoosier state:

> Ignorance and her squalid brood. A universal dearth of intellect. Total abstinence from literature is very generally practiced. . . . Need I stop to remind you of the host of loathsome reptiles such a stagnant pool is fitted to breed! Croaking jealousy; bloated bigotry; coiling suspicion; wormish blindness; crocodile malice!

"Things have changed since then," the narrator concedes, "but in none of the respects mentioned." After alluding to writers who were either driven into exile or destroyed by these conditions, he offers a grim summary: "This Midwest. A dissonance of parts and people, we are a consonance of Towns. Like a man grown fat in everything but heart, we overlabor; our outlook never really urban, never rural either, we enlarge and linger at the same time."

In spite of this dire testimony, Ruth and I chose to come home anyway. We have now lived in the Midwest for twenty-five years, and the literary verdict on our region has not measurably improved. Even though the contemporary Minnesota writer Carol Bly is more charitable than Sinclair Lewis and more hopeful of reform, you can still find in her pages—in *Letters from the Country* (1981), for example, or *The Tomcat's Wife* (1991)—plenty of grudging neighborhoods and savorless people. Another of our contemporaries, Richard Rhodes, says about his hometown of Independence, Missouri: "The town could not have been more midwestern as my adolescence meant the word, rural and shaded and slow, withdrawn behind closed windows and cautious minds."

Warmed-over puritanism, the devotion to property and problem solving, coiling suspicion and cautious minds still dominate the Nebraska towns imagined by Wright Morris in *Plains Song* (1980) and the Iowa farm country depicted by Jane Smiley in *A Thousand Acres* (1991), suggesting that even franchises and televisions and interstate highways have not redeemed the Midwest. In Morris's novel, a woman called back home by a family emergency gazes at her old landscape from a train:

> The dip and rise of the telephone lines, which she had once found so distracting, seemed wearisome and monotonous to her, like the click of the rails. It might have been an abandoned country. Even the towns seemed curiously vacant. It seemed incomprehensible to Sharon that people continued to live in such places. Numbed by the cold, drugged by the heat and the chores, they were more like beasts of the field than people.

At the end of her visit, she feels "an inexpressible relief" as the train begins to carry her away from the "ceaseless humiliations, inadmissible longings, the perpetual chores and smoldering furies, the rites and kinships with half-conscious people so friendly and decent it shamed her to dislike them."

The catalog of regional flaws has changed precious little over the years. The town of Medallion, Ohio, in Toni Morrison's *Sula* (1973) seems hardly more congenial to thought or imagination than Flat Crick, Indiana, from *The Hoosier School-Master* of a century before. Filled with back roads and backwaters such as Flat Crick, Medallion, Spoon River, Gopher Prairie, Black Hawk, and Zenith, the literary baedeker of the Heartland would attract few tourists.

❧

If Midwestern places are so grim and gray, why do writers keep recalling them, sometimes after decades of living far away? What draws imagination back across the miles and years?

The chief lure is the country itself: the forests, fields, and prairies, the wandering rivers, wide skies, dramatic weather, the creekbeds lined with sycamores and limestone, the grasses and flowers, hawks and hickories, moths and cicadas and secretive deer. Again and again in literature about the Midwest you find a dismal, confining human realm—farm, village, or city—embedded in a mesmerizing countryside. In story after story, the hero or heroine despises the town and loves the land. By turns cruel and comforting, the land holds them, haunts them, lingers in their memory and bones.

So long as Huck and Jim stay on their raft, everything they see is glorious—the tangled woods, the sunrises and sunsets, the starlit nights, the gleaming river—but whenever they climb onto shore and cross paths with people, they run into trouble. Every village and homestead is tainted, by slavery or gossip, by liars and fanatics and drunks, by thugs and prudes, and in the meanest places by murderers and thieves. When Huck resolves in the last paragraph of the novel to light out for the frontier, he is fleeing not only his Aunt Sally's instruction but also the wickedness of every settled place.

In his reminiscences of *Life on the Mississippi* (1883), as in his novels about the Great Valley, Mark Twain shows how memory can cherish a landscape while scorning the inhabitants. Consider this panorama from the swollen river:

> The dense, untouched forest overhung both banks of the crooked little crack, and one could believe that human creatures had never intruded there before. The swinging grape-vines, the grassy nooks and vistas glimpsed as we swept by, the flowering creepers waving their red blossoms from the tops of dead trunks, and all the spendthrift richness of the forest foliage, were wasted and thrown away there.

Wasted, presumably, because there were no citizens to admire the scenery; yet the citizens who soon appear are unworthy of their setting:

Behind other islands we found wretched little farms, and wretcheder
little log-cabins; there were crazy rail fences sticking a foot or two
above the water, with one or two jeans-clad, chills-racked, yellow-
faced male miserables roosting on the top-rail, elbows on knees, jaws
in hands, grinding tobacco and discharging the result at floating chips
through crevices left by lost teeth; while the rest of the family and the
few farm-animals were huddled together in an empty wood-flat riding
at her moorings close at hand.

Here and there in his river country, Mark Twain allows for a
saint—a masterful pilot, a kindly aunt, or loyal Jim himself—but
they only serve to demonstrate, by contrast, the corruption of
ordinary folks.

Visiting his own childhood region of northern Iowa and
southern Dakota in 1887, after a spell of high living in the East,
Hamlin Garland was dismayed by what he saw: "The houses, bare
as boxes, dropped on the treeless plains, the barbed-wire fences
running at right angles, and the towns mere assemblages of flimsy
wooden sheds with painted-pine battlement, produced on me the
effect of an almost helpless and sterile poverty." In the stories of
Main-Travelled Roads that Garland wrote following his visit, the
lush countryside makes every human work seem paltry. Here is the
view, for example, of a young sophisticate "who still took pride in
being a Western man," returning after a long absence to his Iowa
home: "The town caught and held his eyes first. How poor and dull
and sleepy and squalid it seemed! The one main street ended at the
hillside at his left, and stretched away to the north, between two
rows of the usual village stores, unrelieved by a tree or a touch of
beauty." Although the town appears diminished by comparison
with cities back East, the land has lost none of its power:

> Accustomed to the White Mountains, to the Alleghanies, he had
> wondered if these hills would retain their old-time charm. They did. He
> took off his hat to them as he stood there. Richly wooded, with gently
> sloping green sides, rising to massive square or rounded tops with dim

vistas, they glowed down upon the squat little town, gracious, lofty in their greeting, immortal in their vivid and delicate beauty.

Along with the yearning figures in Garland's stories, countless other Midwestern characters look up from desolate streets or gaze out from stuffy rooms at the surrounding land, where they find something worthy of their love.

After a run of bad weather, Alexandra Bergson, the heroine of *O Pioneers!*, considers giving up her Nebraska farm, but then decides to extend the mortgage. "That night she had a new consciousness of the country, felt almost a new relation to it," a relation that has less to do with owning the land than with belonging to it: "She had never known before how much the country meant to her. The chirping of the insects down in the long grass had been like the sweetest music. She had felt as if her heart were hiding down there, somewhere, with the quail and the plover and all the little wild things that crooned or buzzed in the sun."

On the eve of his departure from Winesburg, George Willard goes for a long walk in the nearby orchards and berry fields: "He had been in the midst of the great open place on winter nights when it was covered with snow and only the moon looked down at him; he had been there in the fall when bleak winds blew and on summer evenings when the air vibrated with the song of insects. On the April morning he wanted to go there again, to walk again in the silence." Here is a place without gossip or guile, a place that holds him in a way the town no longer does.

When Carol Kennicott of *Main Street* feels most oppressed by Gopher Prairie, she takes a ride at sunset:

> Mounds of straw, and wheatstacks like bee-hives, stood out in startling rose and gold, and the green-tufted stubble glistened. As the vast girdle of crimson darkened, the fulfilled land became autumnal in deep reds and browns. The black road before the buggy turned to a faint lavender, then was blotted to uncertain grayness. Cattle came in a long line up to the barred gates of the farmyards, and over the resting land was a dark glow.

[34]

To make sure we have noted the contrast with the dismal town, Sinclair Lewis adds that "Carol had found the dignity and greatness which had failed her in Main Street."

Jim Burden, who gives such a gloomy account of Black Hawk in *My Ántonia*, nonetheless feels a deep affection for the country: "I recognized every tree and sandbank and rugged draw. I found that I remembered the conformation of the land as one remembers the modelling of human faces." Even the dyspeptic narrator from *In the Heart of the Heart of the Country*, who caused me unnecessary fret when I moved to Indiana, acknowledges that in spring "the lawns are green, the forsythia is singing," and in autumn "the shade is ample, the grass is good, the sky a glorious fall violet; the apple trees are heavy and red, the roads are calm and empty; corn has sifted from the chains of tractored wagons to speckle the streets with gold and with the russet fragments of the cob, and a man would be a fool who wanted, blessed with this, to live anywhere else in the world."

Hemingway pushed the contrast between desolate human realm and mesmerizing countryside to an extreme in "Big Two-Hearted River." Nick Adams returns from the war in Europe, wounded and shaken, to find that the town near his favorite fishing spot in Michigan's Upper Peninsula has burned, leaving no record of human presence there except a layer of ash; yet the river still flows, and, at a distance, the woods flourish: "Two hundred yards down the hillside the fire line stopped. Then it was sweet fern, growing ankle high, to walk through, and clumps of jack pines; a long undulating country with frequent rises and descents, sandy underfoot and the country alive again." Renewed by contact with the land and its creatures—the trout in the stream, the kingfisher gliding overhead, the lurching grasshoppers—Nick also comes alive again.

Any landscape is made up of particulars—sweet ferns and wheatstacks, this creek and that meadow—and writers who imag-

ine the land with most authority honor the details. Recalling a
farm in central Illinois, the narrator of William Maxwell's novel *So
Long, See You Tomorrow* (1980) says, "I became aware of a richness
that wasn't visual but came from the way the smells were laid on:
dried-out wood, rusting farm machinery, the manure pile, the
pigpen, yarrow, and onion grass, quicklime from the outhouse, in
spring the frost leaving the ground, in summer the hay lying cut in
the fields." Becoming aware of the richness in long-settled, cultivated, often battered and abandoned country is the special calling
of Midwestern writers.

৵

Perhaps the most famous expression of longing for a Midwestern
landscape appears in a book that only mentions the region in its
opening and closing pages. When Nick Carraway, narrator of *The
Great Gatsby* (1925), "came back restless" from the same war that
wounded Nick Adams, he tried living in the "Middle Western
city" where he had grown up. He did not stay long: "Instead of
being the warm center of the world, the Middle West now seemed
like the ragged edge of the universe—so I decided to go East and
learn the bond business." The figure who fascinates Carraway took
the same path, starting out as penniless James Gatz of North
Dakota and transforming himself into millionaire Jay Gatsby of
Long Island.

Near the end of the novel, after Gatsby's ambitions have
wrecked several lives, Carraway becomes disillusioned with the
East, even though he remains "keenly aware of its superiority to
the bored, sprawling, swollen towns beyond the Ohio, with the
interminable inquisitions which spared only the children and the
very old." The indictment of Midwestern towns is familiar, almost
perfunctory, as though Fitzgerald felt there was no need to make
the case; but the accompanying description of a lost landscape is

highly wrought: "When we pulled out into the winter night," Carraway recalls from journeys home with school friends,

> and the real snow, our snow, began to stretch out beside us and twinkle against the windows, and the dim lights of small Wisconsin stations moved by, a sharp wild brace came suddenly into the air. We drew in deep breaths of it as we walked back from dinner through the cold vestibules, unutterably aware of our identity with this country for one strange hour, before we melted indistinguishably into it again.
>
> That's my Middle West—not the wheat or the prairies or the lost Swede towns, but the thrilling returning trains of my youth, and the street lamps and sleigh bells in the frosty dark and the shadows of holly wreaths thrown by lighted windows on the snow. I am part of that, a little solemn with the feel of those long winters, a little complacent from growing up in the Carraway house in a city where dwellings are still called through decades by a family's name. I see now that this has been a story of the West, after all—

Carraway says, meaning by "West" the region he elsewhere calls the Middle West. He goes on to say that he and Gatsby and the other key actors in this drama "were all Westerners and perhaps we possessed some deficiency in common which made us subtly unadaptable to Eastern life." Without the acknowledgment of some deficiency, some complacency, some crippling inhibitions, *The Great Gatsby* would not be a bona fide Midwestern story, nor would it be so typical without Carraway's ambivalence toward the region, half savoring and half regretting his attachment to the land.

Like Fitzgerald's narrator, many characters who identify with the Heartland see the country most clearly from the windows of trains or buses or cars, from the decks of rafts or boats, from horseback or wagon bed or motorcycle, for to a striking degree the literature of the Midwest has been one of arrivals and departures. To take a recent example, the roaming Chippewas in Louise Erdrich's stories, returning to their reservations in the Dakotas or Minnesota, often survey their home ground from the road. "When

I came back to the reservation after my long years gone," Lulu
Nanapush declares in *Love Medicine* (1993),

> I saw the leaves of the poplars applaud high in wind. I saw the ducks
> barrel down, reaching to the glitter of the slough water. Wind chopped
> the clouds to rolls that rose and puffed whiter, whiter. Blue Juneberry,
> tough diamond willow. I watched my own face float over the grass,
> traveling alongside me in the dust of the bus window, and I grinned,
> showed my teeth. They could not cage me anymore.

While Midwestern characters, like the writers who create them,
often experience the human world as a series of cages, they also feel
restored and liberated by contact with the land. In our vagabond
culture we have no ready language for this nurturing link between
person and place, so we speak of majesty and charm, dignity and
fulfillment, a thrill of recognition, applauding poplars and singing
forsythia, the trout leaping, the heart hiding in long grass.

❧

If you notice the stress on fecundity in these literary landscapes, you
can appreciate something of the Midwestern writer's dilemma. For
where is the fear of sexuality or suspicion of the flesh more severe
than here in this juicy region, where corn thrusts skyward and hogs
breed and birds flock and every living thing sprouts and fattens?
During most of our history, the conflict between a farming way of life
and an ascetic religion has divided the Midwestern psyche. Nowhere else in America are fertility and prudery so at odds.

More than any other region, the Midwest has fulfilled our
vision of America as the land of plenty. Here is the mouth of the
cornucopia, overflowing with abundant fruits. Here are the deep
soils, thick timber, rich deposits of coal and oil and ore, the slow-
moving, navigable rivers, the level terrain so easily traversed. "No
power upon earth can shut out the emigrants from that fertile
wilderness which offers resources to all industry, and a refuge from

all want," Tocqueville predicted. "Future events, whatever they may be, will not deprive the Americans of their climate or their inland seas, their great rivers or their exuberant soil." Already in the national mythology by Tocqueville's time, New England was known to be stony, stingy ground, with short growing seasons and withering winters; the South was thin-soiled, poor in minerals, with a fitful prosperity that depended on slavery; the far West was mountainous and dry; while the Midwest was loamy and moist and luxuriant.

Because of its resources and history, and in spite of its home-grown critics, the Midwest would eventually become in our mythology something of an agrarian theme park, a repository for values that Americans wish to preserve but not live by: hard work, honesty, frugality, simplicity, integrity, neighborliness, egalitari-anism, politeness, and decency. There is enough truth in that list of Heartland virtues for the impression to have survived into our own time. "The United States, too, has its heartland mystique," observes the geographer Yi-Fu Tuan:

> In the American version of the myth, authentic America is neither the East coast, with its European connections, nor the West coast, with its propensity for surreal fantasies; rather, it is the solid Middle West. Even today foreign dignitaries are expected to visit an Iowa farm if they want to claim they have seen the real country. Unlike Australia, the core area of the United States is exceptionally fertile. The heartland mystique thus does not conflict with geographic reality.

The mystique may not conflict with geography, but it runs head-on into Midwestern culture, which is the result of imposing a religion that fears the body onto a region that is all body. From the beginnings of our literature, anyone could have written, as Garland did in one of his stories, that "the spring evening air came in, laden with the sweet, suggestive smell of bare ground," but until recently nobody would have dared, in print, to find the smell of bare skin equally suggestive and sweet. The imagination is promiscuous, sensual, earthy—which is why writers chafe against the straitjacket of puritanism, and why they return in memory to Midwestern landscapes long since left behind.

୨ଈ

The dark side of fecundity is wholesale death. Beneath the Midwestern writer's affirmation of the country there is often a shudder, as there must be for anyone who looks wilderness in the teeth. Unprotected by mountains, unbuffered by ocean, the region lies open to violent weather—thunderstorms, blizzards, floods, hail, and relentless wind. The Midwest is the world's prime breeding ground for tornadoes, which arise when humid air from the Gulf of Mexico snarls with cool, dry air from the western deserts. In spite of its generosity, the land was not made for us, and it may kill the unhoused or the unwary.

A shudder usually follows the celebration in Hemingway's treatment of landscape. Nick Adams fishes the sunlit parts of the Big Two-Hearted River, but he dreads the gloomy swamp farther downstream:

> Nick did not want to go in there now. He felt a reaction against deep wading with the water deepening up under his armpits, to hook big trout in places impossible to land them. In the swamp the banks were bare, the big cedars came together overhead, the sun did not come through, except in patches; in the fast deep water, in the half light, the fishing would be tragic.

Critics have blamed this intimation of tragedy on the war, on Hemingway's suicidal impulse, on the boggy unconscious; and no doubt all of those explanations carry some of the truth. But the fishing could also be tragic because in the swamp you might stumble, catch a chill, wander lost, or drown. The river that gives life will also snatch it away.

[40]

In *The Trees* (1940), the first novel of a trilogy about the settling of Ohio, Conrad Richter emphasizes the terror felt by people who moved from open country into the dense hardwood forest. "Everywhere she went the trees stood around her like a great herd of dark beasts," the heroine reflects. "Up and up shot the heavy butts of the live ones. Down and down every which way on the forest floor lay the thick rotting butts of the dead ones. Alive or dead, they were mostly grown over with moss. The light that came down here was dim and green. All day even in the cabin you lived in a green light." That ancient forest appeared to go on forever, and did in fact stretch for hundreds of miles, from the Allegheny Mountains on westward to the prairies. Back east,

the trees seemed tame enough. Out here they were wild trees. Even in the daytime you could feel something was watching you. When you went through the woods it followed sly as a fox and stealthy as a Shawanee. Leave your cabin for a season and it would choke it around with brush. Likely you would find trees growing out of your bed when you got back.

So much fertility, such insistent green light, was no more frightening to the Shawnee than to the fox, but it terrified the offspring of European immigrants, who carried images of a landscape wholly tamed and pruned and obedient.

The great plains in Wright Morris's novels present a terrain that is markedly different from Hemingway's swamp or Richter's forest, yet they arouse in his characters a similar feeling of vulnerability. "The faded sky was like the sky at sea," remarks a character in *The Field of Vision* (1956), "the everlasting wind like the wind at sea, and the plain rolled and swelled quite a bit like the sea itself. Like the sea it was lonely, and there was no place to hide." Caught on the prairie with no place to hide and a storm coming on, the heroine of *Main Street* discovers a "tragic landscape":

The pale snow, the prickles of old stubble, and the clumps of ragged brush faded into a gray obscurity. Under the hillocks were cold shadows. The willows about a farmhouse were agitated by the rising wind, and the patches of bare wood where the bark had peeled away were white as the flesh of a leper. The snowy slews were of a harsh flatness. The whole land was cruel, and a climbing cloud of slate-edged blackness dominated the sky.

The shadow side of the generous land is cold and treacherous, as any writer knows who has witnessed the full cycle of a Midwestern year. From the opening page of *My Ántonia* we hear what it was like to grow up in a prairie town, "buried in wheat and corn, under stimulating extremes of climate: burning summers when the world lies green and billowy beneath a brilliant sky, when one is fairly stifled in vegetation, in the color and smell of strong weeds and heavy harvests; blustery winters with little snow, when the whole country is stripped bare and gray as sheet-iron." Throughout Willa Cather's fiction, the barren country plays counterpoint to the billowy green, as in this description from *O Pioneers!*:

> The variegated fields are all one color now; the pastures, the stubble, the roads, the sky are the same leaden gray. The hedge-rows and trees are scarcely perceptible against the bare earth, whose slaty hue they have taken on. The ground is frozen so hard that it bruises the foot to walk in the roads or in the ploughed fields. It is like an iron country, and the spirit is oppressed by its rigor and melancholy. One could easily believe that in that dead landscape the germs of life and fruitfulness were extinct forever.

In Toni Morrison's town of Medallion from *Sula*, when the world was glazed with ice, children "hugged trees simply to hold for a moment all that life and largeness stilled in glass, and gazed at the sun pressed against the gray sky like a worn doubloon, wondering all the while if the world were coming to an end. Grass stood blade by blade, shocked into separateness by an ice that held for days." The winter landscape in Louise Erdrich's *The Beet Queen* (1986) is no less stark:

The snow came so high that rabbits gnawed the trunks and upper limbs, girdling them completely so that even spring, when new buds should have shown, was a time of death. In the shelterbelts, I came across more of the deer's frail hulks and the banks of the river stank of bleached carp. An old man was found, one who for years had lived alone. He was curled in a large drift beneath his clothesline and his arms were full of towels.

For Cather and Morrison and Erdrich, as for many Midwestern writers, the stripped country is like the skull beneath the flesh, the zero point to which all things eventually return. The Midwest has no monopoly on death, of course, but the frozen sterility of December seems all the more appalling by contrast with the steamy fertility of June. The distance between summer and winter may stand for the extreme poles in our vision of the land—as generous or grudging, lush or lean—and for the full range of our feelings—from rapture to numbness, from fierce attachment to fearful distance.

≥●

How easily our response to the land may shift from one pole to the other is suggested by Carol Kennicott's view of the Minnesota countryside: "She saw the prairie, flat in giant patches or rolling in long hummocks. The width and bigness of it, which had expanded her spirit an hour ago, began to frighten her. It spread out so; it went on so uncontrollably; she could never know it." Dwarfed by "the vastness and emptiness of the land," the village offers poor refuge: "She thought of the coming of the Northern winter, when the unprotected houses would crouch together in terror of storms galloping out of that wild waste. They were so small and weak, the little brown houses. They were shelters for sparrows, not homes for warm laughing people."

The key words here are *uncontrollably* and *unprotected*. The dream of dominating the wilderness, making it safe and pliant and profitable, has haunted our continent since the first colonists made landfall on the Atlantic shore; but not until the rise of industrial technology in the nineteenth century, during the hey-day of Midwestern settlement, was there any real prospect of achieving that dream. The same qualities that made the Heart-land ideal for farming and the founding of towns—rich soils, broad rivers, ample rainfall, level terrain—also made it fertile ground for illusions of mastery. Sane people do not think of conquering a mountain range or a desert; but generations of quite sane people could imagine conquering the grasslands and hardwood forests, clearing the trees and breaking the sod, draining the swamps, damming the rivers, reducing the land to obedience.

The first and most famous expression of that ambition was the grid survey, begun in 1785 and laid out systematically, square mile by square mile, on all the country beyond the Ohio. Here was lucid geometry imposed on messy reality, straight lines running due east and west, north and south, traced indiscriminately over hills and valleys, woods and plains, the whole terrain reduced to real estate. The grid is visible today in the zigzag of roads and fences, the patchwork of fields, the layout of towns and cities, the boundaries of government; and sooner or later the grid shows up in most Midwest-ern books. One sign of the taming of the prairie, for Willa Cather, was that "all the fields were under fence, and the roads no longer ran about like wild things, but followed the surveyed section-lines." In the last decade of the twentieth century, Michael Martone could still take the six-mile-square box as the organizing principle for an anthology of Midwestern essays, which he called *Townships* (1992).

Soon after the survey came the steamboats and canals, the railroads, highways, and factories that turned the Midwest, within two or three generations, into an industrial park. This is the story of the whole continent in miniature, of course, just as the taming

[44]

of the wilderness is the great American theme; but the theme has been played out here in the Heartland with fiercer energy and more bitter disillusionment, I believe, than anywhere else in the United States. Just as Midwesterners have carried to an extreme the suspicion of sexuality, so we have carried to an extreme the drive for domination. Menaced by wildness in our bodies and in the land, we have labored to control nature with a thoroughness and zeal unmatched in any other region.

Settlers in the woodlands immediately unpacked their saws and axes to open clearings. The heroine of *The Trees*, unnerved by the green light and the huge trunks standing around like dark beasts, is elated when she comes across a homesteader's "improvement": "The sky hung free and light overhead. The only thing of the woods left here were the black stumps in the tame wheat patch. The eye could look unhindered now." Farther west, where the eye was all too unhindered, settlers in the grasslands immediately began plowing the sod and raising structures—houses and windmills and barns—to break the endless horizon. Along rivers and creeks, settlers began dredging and channeling, harnessing the water as they harnessed their oxen and horses.

I cannot resist quoting Tocqueville one last time, for he discerned in the young republic a view of the land that has proven to be pathological:

> In Europe, people talk a great deal of the wilds of America, but the Americans themselves never think about them: they are insensible to the wonders of inanimate nature, and they may be said not to perceive the mighty forests which surround them till they fall beneath the hatchet. Their eyes are fixed upon another sight: the American people views its own march across these wilds,—drying swamps, turning the course of rivers, peopling solitudes, and subduing nature. This magnificent image of themselves does not meet the gaze of the Americans at intervals only; it may be said to haunt every one of them in his least as well as in his most important actions, and to be always flitting before his mind.

[45]

For a hundred years or so after the Revolution, this effort seemed heroic. But already by the last quarter of the nineteenth century, the birth time for Midwestern literature, the land was beginning to show its wounds. Mark Twain and Hamlin Garland saw them plainly, on riverbanks and prairies. Early in our own century, Edgar Lee Masters saw the wounds in forests cut down for orchards, orchards cut down for roads, and roads choked with dust from automobiles. During World War I, Booth Tarkington could see a Midwestern boomtown as a festering cancer: "It was heaving up in the middle incredibly; it was spreading incredibly; and as it heaved and spread, it befouled itself and darkened its sky."

In the 1930s, Aldo Leopold perceived the wounds in the former pinelands of Wisconsin, which had been scoured down to sterile sand. By the 1940s, Louis Bromfield could see the damage even in the deep soils of Ohio, where the "tradition and habit was simply that of mining the land." A generation ago, Sigurd Olson recorded the damage in the Boundary Waters of northern Minnesota, and James Wright saw it in his beloved Ohio River, which had become a glorified sewer, a "Tar and chemical strangled tomb." Wright Morris has revealed the wounds through the eyes of displaced characters, such as this elderly woman surveying the site of her former Nebraska farm: "Beyond the tall weeds that edged the road, tree stumps torn out by their roots were heaped at the center of a clearing. The deep pits left in the earth had not been filled. It brought to her mind the craters left by bombs." "There was a turmoil about the landscape," Carol Bly writes of today's Minnesota, "as if it might all turn into a single giant shopping center by morning."

The land cannot be damaged without damaging the inhabitants, as individuals and as communities. "Everywhere, in this manner, the past speaks," writes William Gass about Indiana, "and it mostly speaks of failure. The empty stores, the old signs and dusty fixtures, the debris in alleys, the flaking paint and rusty gutters, the heavy locks and sagging boards: they say the same disagreeable things." Among the disagreeable things they say is that, sooner or later, our settlements will suffer the fate of our ransacked country, with everything profitable turned into dollars and the rest left in ruin.

From the first lines of *Sula*, Toni Morrison shows us the connection between abused land and broken community:

> In that place, where they tore the nightshade and blackberry patches from their roots to make room for the Medallion City Golf Course, there was once a neighborhood. It stood in the hills above the valley town of Medallion and spread all the way to the river. It is called the suburbs now, but when black people lived there it was called the Bottom. One road, shaded by beeches, oaks, maples and chestnuts, connected it to the valley. The beeches are gone now, and so are the pear trees where the children sat and yelled down through the blossoms to passersby.

Gone, gone, gone is the inevitable refrain of any writer who looks beyond the walls of bedroom or boardroom to the land. The rich farm country of Minnesota, according to essayist Paul Gruchow, "is now a kind of desert": "The waterfowl are gone, the raptors are gone, the burrowing animals are gone, the predators are gone. Such insects as remain are learning to become specialists in the two or three domestic crops that now grow there, and the most favored of them, like the grasshoppers, come and go in plagues." The narrator of *A Thousand Acres* tells us that her father's Iowa property is "a whole section, paid for, no encumbrances, as flat and fertile, black, friable, and exposed as any piece of land on the face of the earth." By the end of the novel, those acres have been absorbed into a corporate farm, the latest expression of our drive to simplify the land, where "the fields make no room for houses or barnyards or people. No lives are lived any more within the horizon of your gaze."

Our assault on nature has been all too successful, producing year-round a terrain as barren as winter. Already by 1921, the narrator of *So Long, See You Tomorrow* noticed in Illinois "a change in the landscape. It is now like a tabletop, the trees mostly gone, the hedges uprooted in favor of barbed wire—resulting in more land under cultivation, more money in the bank, but also in a total exposure. Anyone can see what used to be reserved for the eye of the hawk as it wheeled in slow circles." We have wheeled in our own lethal circle. Fearing exposure to the wilds, we have scourged the land so thoroughly that we are now exposed to crowding from our own species, and to the poisonous effects of our ingenuity.

❧

"There seemed to be nothing to see," Jim Burden reports in *My Ántonia* about his first impression of Nebraska, "no fences, no creeks or trees, no hills or fields. If there was a road, I could not make it out in the faint starlight. There was nothing but land: not a country at all, but the material out of which countries are made." Within a few years he finds a very different landscape:

> The old pasture land was now being broken up into wheatfields and cornfields, the red grass was disappearing, and the whole face of the country was changing. There were wooden houses where the old sod dwellings used to be, and little orchards, and big red barns; all this meant happy children, contented women, and men who saw their lives coming to a fortunate issue.

"The changes seemed beautiful and harmonious to me," he adds; "it was like watching the growth of a great man or of a great idea."

By now, on the eve of the third millennium, we know too much about erosion, pollution, extinction of species, overpopulation, and resource depletion, about ozone holes, acid rain, smog, traffic congestion, poverty, homelessness, epidemics, addiction, crime, and numerous other ills to think that the country we have made out of the raw land is beautiful and harmonious. Of all regions in America, the Midwest is the one most easily—if super-ficially—subdued, and therefore the one where the failure of our efforts, the waste of riches, the betrayal of promise is most painfully evident. If the literature of the Midwest began as the story of arrivals and departures, it has evolved into a literature of loss. The more abundant the gifts, the more tragic their squandering.

In early accounts, the inland wilderness seemed bountiful but appalling, and in recent accounts the triumph of human will has come to seem equally appalling. Where then shall we live? What many of us long for is a middle state, an inhabited wilderness. It is what the native peoples had, as nearly as we can tell. The Lakota were at home in the grasslands that daunted Cather's sod-busters, as the Shawnee were at home in the woods that terrified Richter's pioneers. The deepest American dream is not, as boosters and advertisers would have us believe, the hunger for money or fame; it is the dream of settling down, in peace and freedom and cooperation, in the promised land.

❧

Wright Morris observed that his books "are apt to bear, on close examination, the stamp of an object made on the plains." Like the plains, his prose is flat and spare, and so are the speech and emotions of his characters, and, like any lone cottonwood or windmill on the bare land, his human figures are isolated and exposed. It might be said of all the writers I have been considering that their books bear the stamp of objects made in the Midwest. If I had to draw up a short list of regional qualities, I would include flatness, fertility, austerity, conformity, civility—and their oppo-sites. None is unique to the Midwest, of course, since the qualities of any region will be variations on those common to America at large. But the combination is distinctive, arising from geography as much as from history.

What I have presented here is less an argument than a map, and it is inevitably a personal one. No matter how many other writers I quote, my own concerns have guided the selection. I want to know how my region has been inhabited and how it has been imagined, because I am convinced that we need to live in our places more conservingly and more lovingly, and that we can only do so if we see our places more truly. In our books, as in our hearts and minds, we need a much greater knowledge of the earth and the human past, and a deeper regard for other creatures.

While studying classics in university, Jim Burden is moved by a line from Virgil's *Georgics*, which he translates for us: "I shall be the first, if I live, to bring the Muse into my country." A teacher explains that "country" here does not mean nation or province, but the poet's own neighborhood, the fields "sloping down to the river and to the old beech trees with broken tops."

Surely this was Cather's own hope, as it has been the hope of countless writers in this and other regions, each one trying to bring his or her homeland into the great conversation of literature. For reasons that had to do with time and place as well as personality, Cather, like many other Midwesterners, wrote about the lost homeland from a distance. Writers who choose to remain here in America's interior still must swim against the current that has carried so many of our predecessors away.

I have no desire to add to the literature of exile. I believe that we need a literature—as we need a culture—of inhabitation, what Wes Jackson of Kansas calls a new homecoming; we need stories of recovery and reconciliation. We see the beginnings of such a literature in *A Country Year* (1986), by Sue Hubbell, who fights to save her patch of Missouri with a fierceness that "comes from having lived in places where beauty, plants and animals are gone." We see it in the stories and essays of Carol Bly, who warns us about the dangers of living "in enmity against the planet," and who will send a funeral director driving past a leveled woods where uranium prospectors have drilled their holes, and allow him to think "of the whole countryside, nearly with tears in his eyes." And we find promise of a literature of inhabitation in Susan Neville's *Indiana Winter* (1994):

> Out here in the heart of the country we've rationalized every inch of earth—all the straight lines of highway and farm and township—but mystery and wildness still lie waiting deep inside every particle of the world, waiting to whirl or crack or ooze into our ordered lives, whether or not we've prepared for it. And the more we deny it, cover it with concrete and lights, the tighter it crouches until it's as small and ordinary as a tube of toothpaste or as large as a crack in the foundations of the world, and we have to pay attention.

All good writing, everywhere and always, is an act of attention. What most needs our attention now, I believe, is the great community of land—air and water and soil and rock, along with all the creatures, human and otherwise, that share the place. We need to imagine the country anew, no longer as enemy or property or warehouse or launching pad, no longer as a lost homeland to be recalled from a distance, but as our present and future home, a dwelling place to be cared for on behalf of all beings for all time.

SANCTUARY

ﻰ

BIRDS LOOSE THEIR alarm calls as I climb from the car. Beware, beware the animal that goes on two legs. My own legs are stiff from the drive that carried me out of town, through southern Indiana hills, to this nature preserve. I often visit this place called Cedar Bluffs with family or friends, idly, cheerfully, stirred by the mix of motives familiar to anyone who wearies of the human zone and hungers for the land. But this day I come alone, for I need to contend with an ache deeper than weariness or hunger. This day, this midseason of my swift life, this end-time of the millennium, I need to confront despair.

It is early one June morning in a wet summer, which means the trees are lush with leaves, the waist-high grasses ripple with juice, and the meadow I must pass through on my way to the bluff will be alive with mosquitoes, chiggers, and ticks. I pull the gray wool socks up over the cuffs of my jeans, draw tight the laces on my boots, and cross the blacktop road.

As I move from the pavement onto the dirt path, I lurch to avoid stepping on a snake. The rope of muscle jerks and vanishes so quickly into the weeds I barely catch a glimpse of pale brown scales ringed by darker bands, markings that could belong to a watersnake or a copperhead. Either species would bite if pestered, but only the copperhead is venomous. My hammering heart does not care about such distinctions. I shiver. My legs seize up, and will not resume walking for a minute or so. The rush of dread feels clean, pure, old. The fear is ancestral, a reflex that has helped keep our evolutionary string from snapping, but for me it is also personal. At the age of three or four, living on a farm in Tennessee, I stumbled into a nest of snakes and nearly died from the bites. Stabs of pain, swelling, delirium: the least flicker of a scaly body brings up the memory like a splash of nausea in the throat.

I look out over the meadow and gather myself. To my right, beyond a thicket of willows and sumac, I see the glint of Clear Creek, whose occasional floods keep this bottom land from turning to forest. The bluff rises on my left, dense with oak and maple and cedar everywhere except for a broad swath cut by the right-of-way for high-tension lines. I do not want to see the looming poles, the sagging wires, yet there they are, scrawled against the sky, higher and more potent than anything else in sight. A few turkey vultures perch on one of the crossbeams, their wings splayed to catch the early sun, like a row of black shirts hung out to dry.

My country has been at war again. The day's news is worse than any nightmare. I came to this 23-acre refuge oppressed by the frenzy of killing and burning and waste that is ravaging the planet, by the sense of my species—and myself—as monstrous. Sight of the snake has narrowed the focus of my anxiety. Beneath my love of wildness, beneath my respect for other lives, there is this primordial terror. Moving on through the meadow, my thighs stroked by the seedheads of grasses, my ears rattling with the scoldings of birds, I keep checking the trail ahead.

Circles of caution spread around me as I walk. Crickets and frogs fall silent, sparrows and warblers flitter to cover, a deer grazing by the creek hoists the white flag of its tail and bounds away. Against my desire for calm, for innocence, I think of men with machine guns patrolling cities, blocking roads, stalking through woods the world over, their stares like radiation piercing everything in sight. At least some of these armed men must enjoy spreading fear, there are so many of them, and so many of them will shoot when orders are given, will shoot even when no orders are given.

In fairy tales, giants send out tremors of fright with every crashing step and thunderous breath. How far does panic spread from the sound of a chain saw, a snowmobile, an off-road motorcycle? And do the wielders of loud machines feel mighty, rousing panic wherever they go? I recall a boastful bumper sticker that shows up on local trucks:

THOUGH I WALK THROUGH THE VALLEY OF THE SHADOW OF DEATH,
I WILL FEAR NO EVIL,
FOR I AM THE MEANEST SON OF A BITCH IN THE VALLEY.

Many of the same bumpers also display an even briefer summary of this popular faith:

IN GUNS WE TRUST.

Maybe the reason we so relentlessly slaughter animals, fell trees, dam rivers, drain swamps, poison whatever thwarts us, bulldoze and batter and pave, is because we aspire to become giants, to be utterly alone and invincible in the valley, to shove death into the shadows.

Truly, I have come to Cedar Bluffs so that I might escape such thoughts for a spell. I force my attention back to the meadow, and immediately I see an electric-blue dragonfly slicing by, zig and zag, then I realize there are dozens of them, hundreds, the air shimmering with these driven flakes. I stop. A speckled orange butterfly lands near me on the yellow disk of an oxeye daisy, and I notice for the first time that the path is lined with daisies; then I notice blossoms everywhere—the fuzzy white parasols of yarrow, the creamy sacs of bladder campions, the blue trumpets of hairy beardtongues, the orange baubles of jewel weed. I draw a deep breath, and smell the rank, green luxuriance. I suddenly hear, behind the buzz of alarm cries, a glee of birds wooing mates, staking out turf, rehearsing old melodies, their voices oblivious to me.

It is a small awakening, to surface from thoughts of myself and my kind and to rise up into the blooming, darting, singing world. The experience is ordinary, yet each time the waking feels fresh, as though I never quite believe that the creation keeps dancing while I sleep. As I move on, I resolve to stay alert, knowing that I will fail, knowing the resolve itself will cloud the windows of perception and shut me up once again inside the house of thought.

る

Where the trail leaves the meadow and enters the shadows of trees, a yellow plastic sign proclaims this patch of ground to be a sanctuary, and a wooden sign identifies it as being owned and managed by the Nature Conservancy. Every time I come here, I give thanks to the people who loved this place enough to salvage it from the bonfire of development, and who, instead of fencing it off for their private use, have left it open for strangers to visit. Visitors come singly, in whispering pairs, in raucous groups, sometimes dozens a day, and their feet keep the trail from grassing over, yet the land, under all that needful looking, seems undiminished.

I walk on through shadows toward the brightness of the creek. The bank is littered with massive chunks of limestone that have tumbled from the bluff. I choose a slab that juts into the stream near a riffle, where I can listen to water shooshing over rocks, and there I sit.

How long I sit I cannot say, because time lets go of me in the presence of moving water. Leaves and twigs ride the current toward me, wobble through the rapids, glide on. Minnows glimmer in the shallows. The sunlight is filled with swarming insects, gnats and midges and creatures whose names I do not know. I do know something about the rock beneath me, for I have talked with men hereabouts who quarry and carve it. I know this limestone was formed in the bed of an ocean three hundred million years ago, in an age that geologists call the Mississippian. The name pleases me, because my father was from Mississippi, and I was born beside the Mississippi River—which makes both of us kin, after a fashion, with the stone.

It is difficult, while resting on rock that is three hundred million years old, to take very seriously the little human play. It is difficult, in this vibrant place, to believe that nature is in jeopardy from anything that our species could possibly do. A fur of moss fills every hollow; green shoots rise from every crack. Seeds drifting through shafts of light flame up like sparks. Dragonflies slash through the milling insects. Behind me, the bluff hunches darkly under the shade of trees, roots gripping stone. Sycamores lean out over the creek, their trunks matted with sticks from high water. On a mud flat, raccoons have left the translucent husks of crayfish and their own dainty pawprints. Turtles bask on a snag in midstream, four of them, shell leaning against shell like a stack of saucers. The creek pours through its channel, scooping and tossing sunlight, and birds pour song into the air. How could this splendor cease? How could it even falter under our puny assault?

If you take a large enough view, of course, the creation does not appear to be in jeopardy. Nothing that we have done or that we are likely to do will upset the solar system, let alone the galaxy or universe. We are very small fry in a vast ocean. The universe revealed by science has expanded enormously since Pascal was terrified by the eternal silence of infinite spaces, since Wordsworth felt a single spirit rolling through mind and nature, even since Frost, early in our century, saw the moon as a luminary clock hung in the indifferent darkness. Within the past few decades, we have discovered that our sun is a routine star near the outer edge of the

Milky Way, and the Milky Way is only one among a billionfold dusting of galaxies. Over the same period, we have uncovered deeper and deeper layers within matter itself, far below the visible surface, beyond the depths of atoms, beyond electrons and protons, beyond quarks, on diminishingly down. Everywhere we look, out far or in deep, from the clustering of galaxies to the spinning of quarks, we find an intricate order whose laws we may decipher but cannot alter.

And yet, while the great web of the cosmos appears to be invulnerable, the threads of creation that pass through our planet, through our local terrain, through our own guts, have come to seem frail, all too easily frayed or broken. The fabric of habitats, the fibers of nerves, the strands of DNA unravel. This bright thread glistening before me, the sun-dappled creek, no longer runs clear, as it did when settlers named it. The water is murky with topsoil. Mounds of dirty foam gather in the shallows. Tires and bottles and other flotsam dangle from roots exposed along the banks. Less visibly, more dangerously, the water is fouled with fertilizer, pesticides, herbicides, solvents, oil. The Indiana Department of Health announced in today's newspaper, as they have done annually for several years, that no one should eat more than half a pound of fish per week taken from Clear Creek, and that women of child-bearing age and children under eighteen should eat none at all. This particular menace comes from polychlorinated biphenyls, or PCBs, one of the many alphabet chemicals that we manufacture in haste, dump in laziness, and then regret in leisure. Every day we discover new reasons for regretting what our predecessors have done; after we are gone, our children will discover even more reasons to regret what we are doing now.

Oceans laid down this limestone over millions of years; the creek wore through the stone to carve these bluffs over thousands of years; yet we needed only a few years to poison the creek. This is no Cuyahoga River, so filthy it catches fire, no Ruhr Valley, no

Love Canal, not an industrial sewer at all, but an obscure stream in the hills of southern Indiana. That we cannot safely eat the fish from this water is a sign of how far the damage has spread.

Nothing we do will unsettle the universe; everything we do affects the planet. This has always been true, but never before our own time have the effects been so rapid or so far-reaching. Some of our deadliest chemicals are now stored in the fat of penguins in Antarctica, in the eggshells of eagles nesting in Alaska, in the brains of monkeys from the Amazon. Biologists estimate that more than one hundred species of plants and animals are disappearing each *day*, the overwhelming proportion of them due to our actions. The web of life is unraveling more swiftly than at any time since the extinction of the dinosaurs, sixty-five million years ago.

Even here in the presence of water and stone I cannot forget these ruinous facts. Even here I am hounded by what I have seen— the forests cut down, the land worn out, animals flattened on roads, trash piling against fences, oil slicks in puddles, smoke sullying the air.

ঽ

Grief drags me to my feet and hustles me along the trail, as though I might rush beyond reach of this knowledge. I soon come to the end of the bluff, turn away from the creek and round the point, then I climb the slope, moving so rapidly that I do not look for late-blooming columbine, I scarcely notice the lacy ferns, and by the time I emerge onto the crown of the bluff I am panting. From floodplain to summit, rising past several million years of earth's history recorded in limestone, I have seen only a gray blur.

Atop the bluff, wherever fissures open in the rock, cedars and oaks have taken root, and in their shade ferns and mosses and wild roses flourish. I pick my way among the twisted trunks until I come to a ledge that offers a view out over the valley of Clear Creek to the woods and fields beyond. Others have been attracted to this promontory, as witness the cigarette butts, the aluminum rings from beverage cans, the initials gouged into stone, the cinders from pleasure fires. Again I sit, smelling ashes and roses, and again I lose track of time.

Two red-tailed hawks circle before me in the gulf of air, calling back and forth. After his death, my father spoke to me as a red-tailed hawk, so I listen carefully to their sharp cries. Now that I am listening, I hear the grumble of a jet, the sizzle of tires on gravel, the snort of trucks on the highway. I hear a tractor working on a nearby farm—mowing hay, I would guess, judging by the sound and season. My forearms itch from the memory of hoisting bales onto wagons.

From up here I can see the high-tension lines humping away for miles over the hills. Crews from the power company used to bush-hog the right-of-way, but now they come through every few years and spray defoliants. They sprayed here lately, and the cleared swath beneath the sagging wires is brittle brown, a sash of dead trees stretching away to the horizon. I know a man who helped perfect the poisons that were used to destroy the jungles in Vietnam, and thus to deny hiding places to the enemy. It was interesting work, the man told me, a real challenge, and patriotic besides. Without the convenience of chemicals, the first white settlers in this region killed trees by stripping away a girdle of bark around the trunks, then felled the hulks with axes and saws, then shoved the wreckage into a pile and set it afire. I suspect the settlers' impulse was not much different from that of the power company or the army—to defeat the forest, erase the shadows, annihilate everything that might oppose our will.

You would think we had cleared a broad enough space to feel secure. But so long as we imagine nature as a realm apart from us, so long as we see wildness as menacing, so long as we crave absolute safety, comfort, and control, we will never be able to rest.

On my way out here this morning I passed several grunting bulldozers, stacks of blazing logs, freshly scalped fields, acres of new asphalt. If we did not see this assault going on around us every-where, every day, we would recognize it for a kind of madness.

To the east, the horizon is broken by a relay tower, a white mast bearing orange dish antennas, like a steel bouquet. I have no idea what sort of signals those antennas catch and throw. The air is laced with our messages. I awoke this morning at six to a radio news item that set me in motion toward Cedar Bluffs. President Bush, I heard, is in Rio de Janeiro today for the Earth Summit, a conference charged with protecting the environment. Although this is the largest gathering of political leaders in history, our own President has gone there reluctantly, in order to avoid bad public-ity. While in Rio, he will demand the weakening of a treaty designed to slow global warming, and he alone, among over a hundred heads of state, will refuse to sign a treaty aimed at protecting the diversity of life on earth. The radio quoted a White House official who justified these dire actions by saying that the President wishes to protect jobs in America.

Hearing that, I sat up in bed and shut off the radio and felt ashamed for my country, a nation which already consumes more than a quarter of the resources used up each year on the entire planet, which produces more than a quarter of the world's pollu-tion, which has ransacked the natural wealth of a continent in two centuries, and all this for the sake of fewer than five per cent of the world's population.

Do not read the news, Thoreau advises; read the eternities. I hear in such news, if not eternity, at least the rumbling of a glacial greed that may well be crushing everything in its path beyond the lifetime of our grandchildren, beyond the lifetime of any sentences we lay down in books, far, far into the future.

Waking to such news, I could not bear to stay within walls, within the grid of streets, and so I came out here to renew my contact with a durable sanity. You can see that I have failed. There is sanity here, and beauty, but they are giving way under the pressure of our hunger. After living for thousands of generations in tiny settlements surrounded by wilderness, over the past half century humans have reduced wilderness to a scattering of remnants surrounded by our settlements. We draw lines around these few scraps and declare them parks, preserves, sanctuaries. Yet the deed of ownership to Cedar Bluffs, the wooden signs marking the boundaries, the attitude of respect that most visitors bring here, cannot protect this place. A true sanctuary is a sacred refuge, a holy place for worship. But there are no longer any refuges from our devices and desires. We treat nothing as holy except our pleasure and ease. We worship only ourselves.

Leaning down to sniff a wild rose, I smell instead the dew-damp ashes. It is as though we have built a great bonfire, and we are heaping onto it everything we can seize—hawks and herrings, swamps and mountains, rivers and soil. If I open a book written in our time, and I do not hear the crackle of flames, I soon close it again, not because I enjoy the reminder of havoc, but because I cannot take seriously an art that ignores this holocaust. We are quick to condemn our ancestors who ignored slavery or apartheid or pogroms or the abuse of women and children. Those who follow us, and inherit from us a severely damaged world, will surely look back on our time and ask what we were doing while the earth burned.

We are all parties to the devastation. I drove to Cedar Bluffs in a gasoline-powered car. The machine on which I write these words runs on electricity carried by those high-tension lines. The choice is not between innocence and guilt; the choice is between more or less complicity. How much do we drag to the bonfire? How much do we save from the flames?

&

From my lookout, I follow the path on along the rim of the bluff, then steeply back down toward the meadow, where the trail completes a loop. Partway down the slope I am clambering over an outcrop when I detect a flash of movement on the stone. I flinch to a halt, thinking *snake*. Then I see it is a salamander, bright blue stripe down the back and tail, its head cocked up to stare at me. The dark eyes gleam. Its pale throat pulses with breath. After a moment it darts away into a crevice, but for that instant there was a connection between us, a dim exchange, and I felt the force of our shared life. The moment will come back to me this evening when I read a passage from Meister Eckhart:

> if you want the kernel you must break the shell. And therefore if you want to discover nature's nakedness you must destroy its symbols, and the farther you get in the nearer you come to its essence. When you come to the One that gathers all things up into itself, there you must stay.

I have come to Cedar Bluffs in search of nature's nakedness, hoping to be reassured by the grace and force and fleetness of creation; and the salamander has given me a token of that inexhaustible energy.

We cannot extinguish the source. The despair that brought me here is not for nature, which will go on, but for us and our companions. We have squandered so much wealth, have fed so ravenously, and yet our appetite still grows. If we destroy ourselves, and take a million species along with us, new forms of life will arise; but that is little consolation for those who love the given world.

&

As I close the loop of the trail and once more draw near to the road, I think about the snake I glimpsed at the beginning of my walk, and how a sudden fear set my heart pounding. Later today, back home, I will reread the poem in which D. H. Lawrence tells of meeting a snake at the water-trough one hot noon. He admired the creature, "earth-golden from the burning bowels of the earth." He felt honored, as though he had been granted an audience with a god. But then the voices of his education spoke up, telling him to hate the snake, to kill it, and so, as it slithered into a hole, he threw a log at the departing tail.

> And immediately I regretted it.
> I thought how paltry, how vulgar, what a mean act!
> I despised myself and the voices of my accursed human education.

Here on the path, now, I remember only how swiftly Lawrence's wonder turned to contempt, his reverence to hatred.

My own education speaks in me with contradictory voices. Some of those voices tell me that the day's headlines do not belong in literature, that numbers do not mix with words, that science is opposed to art; they tell me that fathers do not return from death in the bodies of red-tailed hawks; they tell me that nature is an alien realm, a warehouse of metaphors and scenery and raw materials; they tell me there is no one holy power that gathers all things into itself, that nothing is sacred apart from our sovereign minds, because God is a fiction we have outgrown. Some of those voices tell me that I should not have followed the loop trail through Cedar Bluffs, but instead should have trampled over the ground wherever my fancy might lead; and they tell me that I should not have stayed on the loop of this narrative, but should have dashed hither and yon, demonstrating my cleverness, dazzling the reader.

I resist these falsehoods with the strength of other voices calling to me, the voices of books and teachers and friends, of my own biology, of my soul. The books I live by, the teachers I honor, and the friends I seek are ones that return me to the creation with new awareness and respect. From the confusion of urges that are coiled in my genes, I welcome those that move me to taste the world without devouring it. And what of my soul? I use that antique word for lack of a better one, to point toward the feeling inwardness that binds me to salamander and oxeye daisy and snake, the same inwardness that binds me, friend or stranger, to you.

I have stayed on the trail through Cedar Bluffs so as not to bruise this fragile ground, and I have stayed on the loop of narrative so that you who read this might walk along with me. For what we need, all of us who go on two legs, is to reimagine our place in creation. We need to enlarge our conscience so as to bear, moment by moment, a regard for the integrity and bounty of the earth. There can be no sanctuaries unless we regain a deep sense of the sacred, no refuges unless we feel a reverence for the land, for soil and stone, water and air, and for all that lives. We must find the desire, the courage, the vision to live sanely, to live considerately, and we can only do that together, calling out and listening, listening and calling out.

THE COMMON LIFE

ﬁ

ONE DELICIOUS AFTERNOON while my daughter Eva was home from college for spring vacation, she invited two neighbor girls to help her make bread. The girls are sisters, five-year-old Alexandra and ten-year-old Rachel, both frolicky, with eager dark eyes and shining faces. They live just down the street from us here in Bloomington, Indiana, and whenever they see me pass by, on bicycle or on foot, they ask about Eva, whom they adore.

I was in the yard that afternoon mulching flower beds with compost, and I could hear the girls chattering as Eva led them up the sidewalk to our door. I had plenty of other chores to do in the yard, where every living thing was urgent with April. But how could I stay outside, when so much beauty and laughter and spunk were gathered in the kitchen?

I kept looking in on the cooks, until Eva finally asked, "Daddy, you wouldn't like to knead some dough, would you?"

"I'd love to," I said. "You sure there's room for me?"

"There's room," Eva replied, "but you'll have to wash in the basement."

Hands washed, I took my place at the counter beside Rachel and Alexandra, who perched on a stool I had made for Eva when

[65]

she was a toddler. Eva had still needed that stool when she learned to make bread on this counter; and my son, now six feet tall, had balanced there as well for his own first lessons in cooking. I never needed the stool, but I needed the same teacher—my wife Ruth, a woman with eloquent fingers.

Our kitchen is small; Ruth and I share that cramped space by moving in a kind of dance we have been practicing for years. When we bump one another, it is usually for the pleasure of bumping. But Eva and the girls and I jostled like birds too numerous for a nest. We spattered flour everywhere. We told stories. We joked. All the while I bobbed on a current of bliss, delighting in the feel of live dough beneath my fingers, the smell of yeast, the piping of child-voices so much like the birdsong cascading through our open windows, the prospect of whole-wheat loaves hot from the oven.

An artist might paint this kitchen scene in pastels for a poster, with a tender motto below, as evidence that all is right with the world. All is manifestly *not* right with the world. The world, most of us would agree, is a mess: rife with murder and mayhem, abuse of land, extinction of species, lying and theft and greed. There are days when I can see nothing but a spectacle of cruelty and waste, and the weight of dismay pins me to my chair. On such days I need a boost merely to get up, uncurl my fists, and go about my work. The needed strength may come from family, from neighbors, from a friend's greeting in the mail, from the forked leaves of larkspur breaking ground, from rainstorms and music and wind, from the lines of a handmade table or the lines in a well-worn book, from the taste of an apple or the brash trill of finches in our backyard trees. Strength also comes to me from memories of times when I have felt a deep and complex joy, a sense of being exactly where I should be and doing exactly what I should do, as I felt on that breadmaking afternoon.

I wish to reflect on the sources of that joy, that sense of being utterly in place, because I suspect they are the sources of all that I find authentic in my life. So much in life seems to me unauthentic, I cannot afford to let the genuine passages slip by without considering what makes them ring true. It is as though I spend my days wandering about, chasing false scents, lost, and then occasionally, for a few ticks of the heart, I stumble onto the path. While making bread with my daughter and her two young friends, I was on the path. So I recall that time now as a way of keeping company with Eva, who has gone back to college, but also as a way of discovering in our common life a reservoir of power and hope.

ȋ

What is so powerful, so encouraging, in that kitchen scene? To begin with, I love my three fellow cooks; I relish every tilt of their heads and turn of their voices. In their presence I feel more alive and alert, as if the rust had been knocked off my nerves. The armor of self dissolves, ego relaxes its grip, and I am simply there, on the breeze of the moment.

Rachel and Alexandra belong to the Abed family, with whom we often share food and talk and festivities. We turn to the Abeds for advice, for starts of plants, for cheer, and they likewise turn to us. Not long ago they received troubling news that may force them to move away, and we have been sharing in their distress. So the Abed girls brought into our kitchen a history of neighborliness, a history all the more valuable because it might soon come to an end.

The girls also brought a readiness to learn what Eva had to teach. Eva, as I mentioned, had learned from Ruth how to make bread, and Ruth had learned from a Canadian friend, and our friend had learned from her grandmother. As Rachel and Alexandra shoved their hands into the dough, I could imagine the rope of knowledge stretching back and back through generations, to folks who ground their grain with stones and did their baking in wood stoves or fireplaces or in pits of glowing coals.

If you have made yeast bread, you know how at first the dough clings to your fingers, and then gradually, as you knead in more flour, it begins to pull away and take on a life of its own, becoming at last as resilient as a plump belly. If you have not made yeast bread, no amount of hearing or reading about it will give you that knowledge, because you have to learn through your body, through fingers and wrists and aching forearms, through shoulders and back. Much of what we know comes to us that way, passed on from person to person, age after age, surviving in muscle and bone. I learned from my mother how to transplant a seedling, how to sew on a button; I learned from my father how to saw a board square, how to curry a horse, how to change the oil in a car. The pleasure I take in sawing or currying, in planting or sewing, even in changing oil, like my pleasure in making bread, is bound up with the affection I feel for my teachers and the respect I feel for the long, slow accumulation of knowledge that informs our simplest acts.

Those simple acts come down to us because they serve real needs. You plant a tree or sweep a floor or rock a baby without asking the point of your labors. You patch the roof to stop a leak, patch a sweater to keep from having to throw it out. You pluck the banjo because it tickles your ears and rouses Grandpa to dance. None of us can live entirely by such meaningful acts; our jobs, if nothing else, often push us through empty motions. But unless at least some of what we do has a transparent purpose, answering not merely to duty or fashion but to actual needs, then the heart has gone out of our work. What art could be more plainly valuable than cooking? The reason for baking bread is as palpable as your tongue. After our loaves were finished, Eva and I delivered two of them to the Abeds, who showed in their faces a perfect under-standing of the good of bread.

When I compare the dough to a plump belly, I hear the sexual overtones, of course. By making the comparison, I do not wish to say, with Freud, that every sensual act is a surrogate for sex; on the contrary, I believe sex comes closer to being a stand-in, rather brazen and obvious, like a ham actor pretending to be the whole show, when it is only one player in the drama of our sensual life. That life flows through us constantly, so long as we do not shut ourselves off. The sound of birds and the smell of April dirt and the brush of wind through the open door were all ingredients in the bread we baked.

Before baking, the yeast was alive, dozing in the refrigerator. Scooped out of its jar, stirred into warm water, fed on sugar, it soon bubbled out gas to leaven the loaves. You have to make sure the water for the yeast, like milk for a baby, is neither too hot nor too cold, and so, as for a baby's bottle, I test the temperature on my wrist. The flour, too, had been alive not long before as wheat thriving in sun and rain. Our nourishment is borrowed life. You need not be a Christian to feel, in a bite of bread, a sense of communion with the energy that courses through all things. The lump in your mouth is a chunk of earth; there is nothing else to eat. In our house we say grace before meals, to remind ourselves of that gift and that dependence.

The elements of my kitchen scene—loving company, neighborliness, inherited knowledge and good work, shared purpose, sensual delight, and union with the creation—sum up for me what is vital in community. Here is the spring of hope I have been led to by my trail of bread. In our common life we may find the strength not merely to carry on in face of the world's bad news, but to resist cruelty and waste. I speak of it as common because it is ordinary, because we make it together, because it binds us through time to the rest of humanity and through our bodies to the rest of nature. By honoring this common life, nurturing it, carrying it steadily in mind, we might renew our households and neighborhoods and cities, and in doing so might redeem ourselves from the bleakness of private lives spent in frenzied pursuit of sensation and wealth.

ᴥ

Ever since the eclipse of our native cultures, the dominant American view has been more nearly the opposite: that we should cultivate the self rather than the community; that we should look to the individual as the source of hope and the center of value, while expecting hindrance and harm from society.

What other view could have emerged from our history? The first Europeans to reach America were daredevils and treasure seekers, as were most of those who mapped the interior. Many colonists were renegades of one stripe or another, some of them religious nonconformists, some political rebels, more than a few of them fugitives from the law. The trappers, hunters, traders, and freebooters who pushed the frontier westward seldom recognized any authority beyond the reach of their own hands. Coast to coast, our land has been settled and our cities have been filled by generations of immigrants more intent on leaving behind old tyrannies than on seeking new social bonds.

Our government was forged in rebellion against alien control. Our economy was founded on the sanctity of private property, and thus our corporations have taken on a sacred immunity through being defined under the law as persons. Our criminal justice system is so careful to protect the rights of individuals that it may require years to convict a bank robber who killed a bystander in front of a crowd, or a bank official who left a trail of embezzlement as wide as the Mississippi.

Our religion has been marked by an evangelical Protestantism that emphasizes personal salvation rather than social redemption. To "Get Right with God," as signs along the roads here in the Midwest gravely recommend, does not mean to reconcile your

[70]

fellow citizens to the divine order, but to make a separate peace, to look after the eternal future of your own singular soul. True, we have a remarkable history of communal experiments, most of them religiously inspired—from Plymouth Colony, through the Shaker villages, Robert Owen's New Harmony, the settlements at Oneida, Amana, and countless other places, to the communes in our own day. But these are generally known to us, if they are known at all, as utopian failures.

For much of the present century, Americans have been fighting various forms of collectivism—senile empires during World War I, then Nazism, communism, and now fundamentalist theocracies—and these wars, the shouting kind as well as the shooting kind, have only strengthened our commitment to individualism. We have understood freedom for the most part negatively rather than positively, as release from constraints rather than as the condition for making a decent life in common. Hands off, we say; give me elbow room; good fences make good neighbors; my home is my castle; don't tread on me. I'm looking out for number one, we say; I'm doing my own thing. We have a Bill of Rights, which protects each of us from a bullying society, but no Bill of Responsibilities, which would oblige us to answer the needs of others.

Even where America's founding documents clearly address the public good, they have often been turned to private ends. Consider just one notorious example, the Second Amendment to the Constitution:

A well regulated Militia, being necessary to the security of a free State, the right of the people to keep and bear Arms, shall not be infringed.

It would be difficult to say more plainly that arms are to be kept for the sake of a militia, and a militia is to be kept for defense of the country. In our day, a reasonable person might judge that the Pentagon deploys quite enough weapons, without requiring any supplement from household arsenals. Yet this lucid passage has been construed to justify a domestic arms race, until we now have in America more gun shops than gas stations, we have nearly as many handguns as hands, and we have concentrated enough firepower in the average city to carry on a war—which is roughly what, in some cities, is going on. Thus, by reading the Second Amendment through the lens of our obsessive individualism, we have turned a provision for public safety into a guarantee of public danger.

Observe how zealously we have carved up our cities and paved our land and polluted our air and burned up most of the earth's petroleum within a single generation—all for the sake of the automobile, a symbol of personal autonomy even more potent than the gun. There is a contemptuous ring to the word "mass" in mass transportation, as if the only alternative to private cars were cattle cars. Motorcycles and snowmobiles and three-wheelers fill our public lands with the din of engines and tear up the terrain, yet any effort to restrict their use is denounced as an infringement of individual rights. Millions of motorists exercise those rights by hurling the husks of their pleasures onto the roadside, boxes and bottles and bags. Ravines and ditches in my part of the country are crammed with rusty cars and refrigerators, burst couches and stricken TVs, which their former owners would not bother to haul to the dump. Meanwhile, advertisers sell us everything from jeeps to jeans as tokens of freedom, and we are so infatuated with the sovereign self that we fall for the spiel, as if by purchasing one of a million identical products we could distinguish ourselves from the herd.

The cult of the individual shows up everywhere in American lore, which celebrates drifters, rebels, and loners, while pitying or reviling the pillars of the community. The backwoods explorer like Daniel Boone, the riverboat rowdy like Mike Fink, the lumberjack, the prospector, the rambler and gambler, the daring crook like Jesse James and the resourceful killer like Billy the Kid, along with countless lonesome cowboys, all wander, unattached, through the great spaces of our imagination. When society begins to close in, making demands and asking questions, our heroes hit the road. Like Huckleberry Finn, they are forever lighting out for the Territory, where nobody will tell them what to do. Huck Finn ran away from what he called civilization in order to leave behind the wickedness of slavery, and who can blame him, but he was also running away from church and school and neighbors, from aunts who made him wash before meals, from girls who cramped his style, from chores, from gossip, from the whole nuisance of living alongside other people.

In our literature, when community enters at all, it is likely to appear as a conspiracy against the free soul of a hero or heroine. Recall how restless Natty Bumppo becomes whenever Cooper drags him in from the woods to a settlement. Remember how strenuously Emerson preaches against conforming to society and in favor of self-reliance, how earnestly Hawthorne warns us about the tyranny of those Puritan villages. Think of Thoreau running errands in Concord, rushing in the front door of a house and out the back, then home to his cabin in the woods, never pausing, lest he be caught in the snares of the town. Think of the revulsion Edna Pontellier feels toward the Creole society of New Orleans in Kate Chopin's *The Awakening*. Think of Willa Cather's or Toni Morrison's or James Baldwin's high-spirited women and men who can only thrive by fleeing their home communities. Think of Spoon River, Winesburg, Gopher Prairie, Zenith, all those oppressive fictional places, the backward hamlets and stifling suburbs and heartless cities that are fit only for drones and drudges and mindless Babbitts.

In *The Invasion of the Body Snatchers*, a film from my childhood that still disturbs my dreams, an alien life form takes over one person after another in a small town, merging them into a single creature with a single will, until just one freethinking individual remains, and even he is clearly doomed. Along with dozens of other invasion tales, the film was a warning against communism, I suppose, but it was also a caution against the perils of belonging, of losing your one sweet self in the group, and thus it projected a fear as old as America.

Of course you can find American books and films that speak as passionately for the virtues of our life together as for the virtues of our lives apart. To mention only a few novels from the past decade, I think of Gloria Naylor's *Mama Day*, Wendell Berry's *A Place on Earth*, Ursula Le Guin's *Always Coming Home*, and Ernest Gaines's *A Gathering of Old Men*. But they represent a minority opinion. The majority opinion fills bestseller lists and cinema screens and billboards with isolated, alienated, rebellious figures who are too potent or sensitive for membership in any group.

ᨠ

I have been shaped by this history, and I, too, am uneasy about groups, especially large ones, above all those that are glued together by hatred, those that use a color of skin or a cut of clothes for admission tickets, and those that wrap themselves in scriptures or flags. I have felt a chill from blundering into company where I was not wanted. I have known women and men who were scorned because they refused to fit the molds their neighbors had prepared for them. I have seen Klansmen parading in white hoods, their crosses burning on front lawns. I have seen a gang work its way through a subway car, picking on the old, the young, the weak. Through film I have watched the Nuremberg rallies, watched policemen bashing demonstrators in Chicago, missiles parading in Red Square, tanks crushing dissidents in Tiananmen Square. Like everyone born since World War II, I have grown up on television images of atrocities carried out, at home and abroad, with the blessing of governments or revolutionary armies or charismatic thugs.

[74]

In valuing community, therefore, I do not mean to approve of any and every association of people. Humans are drawn together by a variety of motives, some of them worthy, some of them ugly. Anyone who has spent recess on a school playground knows the terror of mob rule. Anyone who has lived through a war knows that mobs may pretend to speak for an entire nation. I recently saw, for the first time in a long while, a bumper sticker that recalled for me the angriest days of the Vietnam War: AMERICA—LOVE IT OR LEAVE IT. What loving America seemed to mean, for those who brandished that slogan back around 1970, was the approval of everything the government said or the army did in our name. "All those who seek to destroy the liberty of a democratic nation ought to know," Alexis de Tocqueville observed in *Democracy in America,* "that war is the surest and the shortest means to accomplish it." As a conscientious objector, with a sister who studied near my home in Ohio on a campus where National Guardsmen killed several protesters, I felt the force of despotism in that slogan.

Rather than give in to despotism, some of my friends went to jail and others into exile. My wife and I considered staying in England, where we had been studying for several years and where I had been offered a job. But instead we chose to come home, here to the Midwest where we had grown up, to work for change. In our idealism, we might have rephrased that bumper sticker to read: AMERICA—LOVE IT AND REDEEM IT. For us, loving America had little to do with politicians and even less with soldiers, but very much to do with what I have been calling the common life: useful work, ordinary sights, family, neighbors, ancestors, our fellow creatures, and the rivers and woods and fields that make up our mutual home.

During the more than twenty years since returning to America, I have had some of the idealism knocked out of me, but I still believe that loving your country or city or neighborhood may require you to resist, to call for change, to speak on behalf of what you believe in, especially if what you believe in has been neglected.

What we have too often neglected, in our revulsion against tyranny and our worship of the individual, is the common good. The results of that neglect are visible in the decay of our cities, the despoiling of our land, the fouling of our rivers and air, the haphazard commercial sprawl along our highways, the gluttonous feeding at the public trough, the mortgaging of our children's and grandchildren's future through our refusal to pay for current consumption. Only a people addicted to private pleasure would allow themselves to be defined as consumers—rather than conservers or restorers—of the earth's abundance.

In spite of the comforting assurances, from Adam Smith onward, that the unfettered pursuit of private wealth should result in unlimited public good, we all know that to be mostly a lie. If we needed reminders of how great that lie is, we could look at the savings and loan industry, where billions of dollars were stolen from small investors by rich managers who yearned to be richer; we could look at the Pentagon, where contracts are routinely encrusted with graft, or at Wall Street, where millionaires finagle to become billionaires through insider trading; we could look at our national forests, where logging companies buy timber for less than the cost to taxpayers of harvesting it; or we could look at our suburbs, where palaces multiply, while downtown more and more people are sleeping in cardboard boxes. Wealth does not precipitate like dew from the air; it comes out of the earth and from the labor of many hands. When a few hands hold onto great wealth, using it only for personal ease and display, that is a betrayal of the common life, the sole source of riches.

❧

Fortunately, while our tradition is heavily tilted in favor of private life, we also inherit a tradition of caring for the community. Although Tocqueville found much to fear and quite a bit to despise in this raw democracy, he praised Americans for having "carried to the highest perfection the art of pursuing in common the object of their common desires." Writing of what he had seen in the 1830s, Tocqueville judged Americans to be avaricious, self-serving, and aggressive; but he was also amazed by our eagerness to form clubs, to raise barns or town halls, to join together in one cause or another: "In no country in the world, do the citizens make such exertions for the common weal. I know of no people who have established schools so numerous and efficacious, places of public worship better suited to the wants of the inhabitants, or roads kept in better repair."

Today we might revise his estimate of our schools or roads, but we can still see all around us the fruits of that concern for the common weal—the libraries, museums, courthouses, hospitals, orphanages, universities, parks, on and on. Born as most of us are into places where such amenities already exist, we may take them for granted; but they would not be there for us to use had our forebears not cooperated in building them. No matter where we live, our home places have also benefited from the Granges and unions, the volunteer fire brigades, the art guilds and garden clubs, the charities, food kitchens, homeless shelters, soccer and baseball teams, the Scouts and 4-H, the Girls and Boys Clubs, the Lions and Elks and Rotarians, the countless gatherings of people who saw a need and responded to it.

This history of local care hardly ever makes it into our literature, for it is less glamorous than rebellion, yet it is a crucial part of our heritage. Any of us could cite examples of people who dug in and joined with others to make our home places better places. Women and men who invest themselves in their communities, fighting for good schools or green spaces, paying attention to where they are, seem to me as worthy of celebration as those adventurous loners who keep drifting on, prospecting for pleasure.

A few days after our breadmaking, Eva and I went to a concert in Bloomington's newly opened arts center. The old limestone building had once been the town hall, then a fire station and jail, then for several years an abandoned shell. Volunteers bought the building from the city for a dollar, then renovated it with materials, labor, and money donated by local people. Now we have a handsome facility that is in constant use for pottery classes, theater productions, puppet shows, art exhibits, poetry readings, and every manner of musical event.

The music Eva and I heard was *Hymnody of Earth*, for hammer dulcimer, percussion, and children's choir. Composed by our next-door neighbor, Malcolm Dalglish, and featuring lyrics by our Ohio Valley neighbor, Wendell Berry, it was performed that night by Malcolm, percussionist Glen Velez, and the Bloomington Youth Chorus. As I sat there with Eva in a sellout crowd—about a third of whom I knew by name, another third by face—I listened to music that had been elaborated within earshot of my house, and I heard my friend play his instrument, and I watched those children's faces shining with the colors of the human spectrum, and I felt the restored building clasping us all like the cupped hands of our community. I knew once more that I was in the right place, a place created and filled and inspired by our lives together.

੨੦

A woman who recently moved from Los Angeles to Bloomington told me that she would not be able to stay here long, because she was already beginning to recognize people in the grocery stores, on the sidewalks, in the library. Being surrounded by familiar faces made her nervous, after years in a city where she could range about anonymously. Every traveler knows the sense of liberation that comes from journeying to a place where nobody expects anything of you. Everyone who has gone to college knows the exhilaration of slipping away from the watchful eyes of Mom and Dad. We all need seasons of withdrawal from responsibility. But if we make a career of being unaccountable, we have lost something essential to our humanity, and we may well become a burden or a threat to those around us. A community can support a number of people who are just passing through, or who care about no one's needs but their own; the greater the proportion of such people, however, the more vulnerable the community, until eventually it breaks down. That is true on any scale, from a household to a planet.

The words *community*, *communion*, and *communicate* all derive from *common*, and the two syllables of *common* grow from separate roots, the first meaning "together" or "next to," the second having to do with barter or exchange. Embodied in that word is a sense of our shared life as one of giving and receiving—music, touch, ideas, recipes, stories, medicine, tools, the whole range of artifacts and talents. After twenty-five years with Ruth, that is how I have come to understand marriage, as a constant exchange of labor and love. We do not calculate who gives how much; if we had to, the marriage would be in trouble. Looking outward from this community of two, I see my life embedded in ever larger exchanges— those of family and friendship, neighborhood and city, countryside and country—and on every scale there is giving and receiving, calling and answering.

Many people shy away from community out of a fear that it may become suffocating, confining, even vicious; and of course it may, if it grows rigid or exclusive. A healthy community is dynamic, stirred up by the energies of those who already belong, open to new members and fresh influences, kept in motion by the constant bartering of gifts. It is fashionable just now to speak of this open quality as "tolerance," but that word sounds too grudging to me—as though, to avoid strife, we must grit our teeth and ignore whatever is strange to us. The community I desire is not grudging; it is exuberant, joyful, grounded in affection, pleasure, and mutual aid. Such a community arises not from duty or money but from the free interchange of people who share a place, share work and food, sorrows and hope. Taking part in the common life means dwelling in a web of relationships, the many threads tugging at you while also holding you upright.

I have told elsewhere the story of a man who lived in the Ohio township where I grew up, a builder who refused to join the volunteer fire department. Why should he join, when his house was brick, properly wired, fitted out with new appliances? Well, one day that house caught fire. The wife dialed the emergency number, the siren wailed, and pretty soon the volunteer firemen, my father among them, showed up with the pumper truck. But they held back on the hoses, asking the builder if he still saw no reason to join, and the builder said he could see a pretty good reason to join right there and then, and the volunteers let the water loose.

I have also told before the story of a family from that township whose house burned down. The fire had been started accidentally by the father, who came home drunk and fell asleep smoking on the couch. While the place was still ablaze, the man took off, abandoning his wife and several young children. The local people sheltered the family, then built them a new house. This was a poor township. But nobody thought to call in the government or apply to a foundation. These were neighbors in a fix, and so you helped them, just as you would harvest corn for an ailing farmer or pull a flailing child from the creek or put your arm around a weeping friend.

I am not harking back to some idyllic past, like the one embalmed in the *Saturday Evening Post* covers by Norman Rockwell or the prints of Currier and Ives. The past was never golden. As a people, we still need to unlearn some of the bad habits formed during the long period of settlement. One good habit we might reclaim, however, is that of looking after those who live nearby. For much of our history, neighbors have kept one another going, kept one another sane. Still today, in town and country, in apartment buildings and barrios, even in suburban estates, you are certain to lead a narrower life without the steady presence of neighbors. It is neither quaint nor sentimental to advocate neighborliness; it is far more sentimental to suggest that we can do without such mutual aid.

Even Emerson, preaching self-reliance, knew the necessity of neighbors. He lived in a village, gave and received help, and delivered his essays as lectures for fellow citizens whom he hoped to sway. He could have left his ideas in his journals, where they first took shape, but he knew those ideas would only have effect when they were shared. I like to think he would have agreed with the Lakota shaman, Black Elk, that "a man who has a vision is not able to use the power of it until after he has performed the vision on earth for the people to see." If you visit Emerson's house in Concord, you will find leather buckets hanging near the door, for he belonged to the village fire brigade, and even in the seclusion of his study, in the depths of thought, he kept his ears open for the alarm bell.

We should not have to wait until our houses are burning before we see the wisdom of facing our local needs by joining in common work. We should not have to wait until gunfire breaks out in our schools, rashes break out on our skin, dead fish float in our streams, or beggars sleep on our streets before we act on behalf of the community. On a crowded planet, we had better learn how to live well together, or we will live miserably apart.

❧

In cultural politics these days there is much talk of diversity and difference. This is all to the good, insofar as it encourages us to welcome the many distinctive traditions and visions that have flowed into America from around the world. But if, while respecting how we differ, we do not also recognize how much we have in common, we will have climbed out of the melting pot into the fire. Every day's newspaper brings word of people suffering and dying in the name of one distinction or another. We have never been slow to notice differences—of accent, race, dress, habits. If we merely change how those differences are valued, celebrating what had formerly been despised or despising what had been celebrated, we continue to define ourselves and one another in the old divisive ways.

Ethnic labels are especially dangerous, for, while we pin them on as badges of pride, we may have difficulty taking them off when others decide to use them as targets. The larger the group identified by a label, the less likely it is to be a genuine community. Haste or laziness may lead us to speak of blacks and whites, of Christians and Muslims and Jews, of Armenians and Mexicans, yet the common life transcends such categories. Sharing a national anthem, a religion, or a skin color may be grounds for holding rallies or waging war, but community is more intimate than nationality, more subtle than race or creed, arising not from abstract qualities but from the daily give-and-take among particular people in a particular place.

It is also dangerous to separate a concern for human diversity from a concern for natural diversity. Since Europeans arrived in North America, we have been drawing recklessly on beaver and bison, trees and topsoil, petroleum, coal, iron and copper ore, clean air and water. Many of the achievements on which we pride ourselves are the result not of our supposed virtues but of this plundered bounty. We do not have another continent to use up; unless we learn to inhabit this one more conservingly, we will see our lives, as well as the land, swiftly degraded. There is no contradiction between caring for our fellow human beings and caring for the rest of nature; on the contrary, only by attending to the health of the land can we measure our true needs or secure a lasting home.

Just before Eva was to leave again for college, she and I went for a hike in a nature preserve along Clear Creek, near Bloomington, to look at the hepatica and bloodroot and listen to the spring-high water. At the edge of the preserve, a wooden sign declared that the riding of horses was prohibited. The trail had been freshly gouged by horseshoes and was eroding badly. Trash snagged in the roots of sycamores along the stream. Much of the soil and its cover of wildflowers had washed from the slopes where people scrambled up to picnic on the limestone bluff. Some of the cans they had left behind glinted among white stars of trillium.

I wondered what it would take to persuade the riders to get down off their horses and go on foot. What would it take to discourage people from dumping their worn-out washing machines in ditches? What would convince farmers to quit spraying poisons on their fields, suburbanites to quit spraying poisons on their lawns? What power in heaven or earth could stop loggers from seeing every tree as lumber, stop developers from seeing every acre of land as real estate, stop oil-company executives from seeing our last few scraps of wilderness as pay dirt waiting to be drilled? What would it take to persuade all of us to eat what we need, rather than what we can hold; to buy what we need, rather than what we can afford; to draw our pleasure from inexhaustible springs?

Signs will not work that change of mind, for in a battle of signs the billboards always win. Police cannot enforce it. Tongue lashings and sermons and earnest essays will not do it, nor will laws alone bring it about. The framers of the Constitution may have assumed that we did not need a Bill of Responsibilities because religion and reason and the benign impulses of our nature would lead us to care for one another and for our home. At the end of a bloody century, on the eve of a new millennium that threatens to be still bloodier, few of us now feel much confidence in those redeeming influences. Only a powerful ethic might restrain us, retrain us, restore us. Our survival is at stake, yet worrying about

[83]

our survival alone is too selfish a motive to carry us as far as we need to go. Nothing short of reimagining where we are and what we are will be radical enough to transform how we live.

Aldo Leopold gave us the beginnings of this new ethic nearly half a century ago, in *A Sand County Almanac*, where he described the land itself as a community made up of rock, water, soil, plants, and animals—including Homo sapiens, the only species clever enough to ignore, for a short while, the conditions of membership. "We abuse land because we see it as a commodity belonging to us," Leopold wrote. "When we see land as a community to which we belong, we may begin to use it with love and respect." To use our places with love and respect demands from us the same generosity and restraint that we show in our dealings with a wife or husband, a child or parent, a neighbor, a stranger in trouble.

Once again this spring, the seventy-seventh of her life, my mother put out lint from her clothes dryer for the birds to use in building their nests. "I know how hard it is to make a home from scratch," she says, "I've done it often enough myself." That is not anthropomorphism; it is fellow feeling, the root of all kindness.

Doctors the world over study the same physiology, for we are one species, woven together by strands of DNA that stretch back to the beginnings of life. There is, in fact, only one life, one pulse animating the dust. Sycamores and snakes, grasshoppers and grass, hawks and humans all spring from the same source and all return to it. We need to make of this common life not merely a metaphor, although we live by metaphors, and not merely a story, although we live by stories; we need to make the common life a fact of the heart. That awareness, that concern, that love needs to go as deep in us as the feeling we have when a child dashes into the street and we hear a squeal of brakes, or when a piece of our home ground goes under concrete, or when a cat purrs against our palms or rain sends shivers through our bones or a smile floats back to us from another face.

With our own population booming, with frogs singing in the April ponds, with mushrooms cracking the pavement, life may seem the most ordinary of forces, like hunger or gravity; it may seem cheap, since we see it wasted every day. But in truth life is expensive, life is extraordinary, having required five billion years of struggle and luck on one stony, watery planet to reach its present precarious state. And so far as we have been able to discover from peering out into the great black spaces, the life that is common to all creatures here on earth is exceedingly uncommon, perhaps unique, in the universe. How, grasping that, can we remain unchanged?

It may be that we will not change, that nothing can restrain us, that we are incapable of reimagining our relations to one another or our place in creation. So many alarm bells are ringing, we may be tempted to stuff our ears with cotton. Better that we should keep ears and eyes open, take courage as well as joy from our common life, and work for what we love. What I love is curled about a loaf of bread, a family, a musical neighbor, a building salvaged for art, a town of familiar faces, a creek and a limestone bluff and a sky full of birds. Those may seem like frail threads to hold anyone in place while history heaves us about, and yet, when they are braided together, I find them to be amazingly strong.

FAITH AND WORK

Ze

AFTER MAKING DO for twenty years with a gloomy, cramped, inconvenient kitchen, a room designed for trolls, my wife and I have
decided to rip everything out, right back to the studs and joists,
and begin over. Friends who have been through milder remodel-
ings warn us that we are putting our marriage at risk.

"All we did was refinish the cupboards," said a neighbor, "and
my husband and I quit speaking for a month."

The calm, song-writing carpenter whom we have hired to do
the skilled work observes that the only couples he has known to
come through such root-and-branch renovations unscathed are
those who moved out for the duration. Even if we had a place to go,
we could not abandon the house, because my wife and son and I are
going to do as much of the work as our talents and schedules allow.
Besides, I would rather get my hands dirty making over this old
house than keep them clean in some rented place. Compared to
what I do most days—the shuffling of paper and juggling of words—
there is a sweet solidity in tearing out plaster and banging nails.

Like sensible people, my wife and son dread this upheaval. As
soon as hammering begins, passage will be cut off between the
front of the house and the back. In order to raid the refrigerator,

FAITH AND WORK

which he does now with the zeal of a bear visiting a salmon run, Jesse will have to walk outside through the yard. Since the yard is presently buried under nine inches of snow, and since laundry will have to be hauled between upstairs and basement over the same route, Ruth envisions journeys as arduous as those of the voyageurs carrying loads of beaver pelts through the north woods. For a month or so we will be cooking on a hot plate in the bedroom left vacant while our daughter is away at college. We will be fetching food from the back porch, hunting through boxes for herbs and books, washing dishes in the bathtub. There will be sawdust and plaster in every breath, grit in every bite.

On the Sunday before we are to begin demolition, our minister reads from the pulpit the world-weary lines of Ecclesiastes, "For everything there is a season, and a time for every matter under heaven," and when he comes to the fourth item on the list, "a time to break down, and a time to build up," I cannot help thinking of crowbars and hammers.

"You see," I tell Ruth in the car on our way home, "even old Ecclesiastes is in favor of remodeling kitchens."

She points out that the next item on the list, right after a time for breaking down and building up, is a time for weeping.

"Maybe Ecclesiastes just didn't enjoy carpentry," I say.

"Maybe his wife wrote that line," Ruth suggests.

When sensible people dread the prospect, when neighbors warn us of coming strife, when our carpenter shakes his musical head at the looming problems, why do I look forward to this dirty, disruptive, wearying labor? In trying to answer that, I have been thinking about the sorts of work I love.

❧

To love any sort of work may seem an odd emotion in a country where bumper stickers proclaim that WORK IS A FOUR-LETTER WORD.

In late twentieth-century America, our factories fill with robots and our stores with vending machines and our homes with labor-saving gadgets. Judging by how we spend money, we are far more intent on saving our labor than on saving our souls. There are retrograde folks here and there who stubbornly make bread from scratch or dig the garden in spring with a spade or walk up stairs; but far more of us are devoted to the ease of elevators, tractors, and automatic bread-makers. The drift of our society as a whole seems to be toward an electronic garden of Eden, in which all one's needs would be filled through shopping channels or malls, and one's toughest chores would be to push buttons and stare at screens and chew.

When Adam and Eve were kicked out of the original garden, according to the old story, God told them, "cursed is the ground because of you; in toil you shall eat of it all the days of your life; thorns and thistles it shall bring forth to you; and you shall eat the plants of the field. In the sweat of your face you shall eat bread till you return to the ground." On the whole, the descendants of Adam and Eve have done better than to grub out thorns and thistles—which is why there are now nearly six billion of us on the earth. The plants of the field have given us corn and beans, rice and wheat. Yet even these glorious foods do not satisfy us. We crave easier and faster fare—gourmet meals in microwave boxes, drive-in feasts—as though only by entirely avoiding sweat and toil can we undo God's curse. If we are to sweat, we prefer doing so in health spas or on jogging tracks or beaches, an expensive sort of sweat aimed at making us look good in swimsuits rather than in heaven. The less we toil to provide for living, the more we toil to postpone dying.

Even in our push-button nirvana, of course, many people work hard at their jobs and in their homes and on their land, and some of them do so without thinking of work as a curse. Deryl Dale, our kitchen carpenter, gets up at five, drives to a coffee shop for an hour of reading, then labors all day at tearing down and building up, then—depending on the season—helps his wife in her market garden until dark or helps his children with their studies, and on weekends he practices his music. And through it all he is utterly serene.

Over the years I have occasionally met with that union of hard work and serenity in farmers and nurses, welders and cooks, truck drivers, janitors, teachers, mechanics, letter carriers, librarians, lawyers, and clerks. These were people doing what they felt called to do, without looking for an escape, without hankering for smaller tasks or bigger paychecks. Much of the devoted work I've witnessed has had nothing to do with money. I think of my mother painting china plates or carrying flowers to shut-ins. I think of my father stopping to change flat tires for strangers or currying a horse or carving wood. I think of my sister weaving, my daughter studying birds, my wife cooking meals for ailing friends.

My Mississippi grandmother reared eleven children on a farm, and when the youngest of the children had left home, she threw herself into serving her neighbors, and never collected a paycheck in her life. My Assyrian grandfather continued doctoring in Chicago right through the Depression when his patients could not pay him, went bankrupt from giving away medicine, lost everything except his clothes and his instruments, then kept on practicing until he was eighty. "I learned healing," he once told me, "so how can I just fold my hands and quit?"

When I consider the varied personalities of those diligent people, I feel certain that the willingness to work hard without complaint, indeed with gusto, has less to do with temperament than with conviction. If you believe that work is an evil to be avoided, if you aspire to loaf and invite your ease, then you will grab for every labor-saving gimmick, you will dodge every demand for effort, whether on the job or in school or at home, and you will coax or bully others into providing for your needs. But if you believe that work is a calling, a discipline, a way of exercising your gifts, even a way toward God, then work will seem to you as natural, as desirable, as breathing.

ॐ

The building up of our new kitchen began in imagination long before the breaking down of the old one. Ruth and I have spent months drawing plans, trying to fit all our cookery schemes into a space that measures twelve feet by twelve. We draw in pencil, because every time we think the design is perfect, some doorway or appliance or pipe interferes, and we have to wield the eraser. Finally, after wearing holes in many sheets of paper, we agree on a plan.

On Sunday, after hearing the weary words of Ecclesiastes, we clear the way for that plan by stripping our old kitchen to the walls. While Ruth carries dishes and pans and food upstairs to our daughter's bedroom, Jesse and I undo the connections for gas and water and electricity. We take out the refrigerator, the dishwasher, the stove, the sink, then we unscrew the counters and cupboards and lug them to the basement. By late afternoon, the empty room echoes our footsteps, and my back flares with pain.

I lie down on the kitchen floor and press my spine flat against the scuffed linoleum. Jesse looms above me, unbent, hands on hips, surveying the bare walls, the dangling wires, the amputated pipes.

"We did it, buddy," I tell him.

"We sure did," he answers.

The chill of the linoleum soothes my back. Then I groan, remembering the nine inches of snow.

"What's the matter?" Jesse asks.

"Deryl's going to need a path down the driveway when he starts work tomorrow." I close my eyes, and before I can open them, I hear Jesse clumping down the steps.

When I call him in for supper, I see that he has not only

cleared snow from the driveway but has kept on shoveling to our back door, across the yard to our compost bin, and across our neighbors' yard to their porch.

"Thanks," I tell him. "That was a big job."

"What?"

"All the shoveling."

"Oh," he says. "That. Yeah. No problem."

My mother and several friends join us for supper, to help celebrate the beginning of our labor. Ruth dishes out stir-fry onto our plates, and the fragrance of sesame oil makes me forget the pain in my back.

"How do you like cooking in a bedroom?" I ask Ruth.

"It reminds me of camping out," she answers. "I suppose it will get old before too long, but so far it's kind of fun."

Telling our guests about all that we accomplished that day, I lather myself into a sermon on the joys of doing good work for its own sake, without regard to applause or pay. After I wind down, my mother recalls that when I was in first grade I made boats from scrap wood in my father's shop, then sold them to classmates for a nickel apiece. "You can see he's getting less mercenary with age," my mother concludes. I do not remember the nickels, but I remember making the boats. Getting the curves on the two sides of the bow to match and drilling straight holes for the chimneys were the hardest parts.

"So Jesse," one of our friends asks, "how much do you get per hour for helping your old man?"

"About five cents less than a nickel," Jesse answers. "But at least he isn't charging me for the experience."

❧

Opus, the Latin word that we apply to musical compositions, has the twin meanings of work and riches. We hear it in operate and *opulence.* Good work enriches the world and also enriches the worker; it draws on our creativity, our ability to imagine actions before carrying them out, and our freedom to act on those images, guided by intelligence and skill. The medieval guilds of carpenters, weavers, dyers, and millers spoke of their trades as mysteries. The skills passed down from master to apprentice were powerful legacies. In our time, assembly lines and bureaucracies substitute procedures for intelligence and transfer skills to machines. The difference between a machine and a tool—between a bread-maker and a bread pan—is that a tool extends human skills, a machine replaces them. When the freedom and craft have been squeezed out of work it becomes toil, without mystery or meaning, and that is why many people hate their jobs. You can measure the drudgery of a job by the number of layers of supervision required to keep the wheels spinning or the cash registers ringing. Toil drains us; but good work may renew us, by giving expression to our powers.

Work shapes our body, fills our thoughts and speech, stamps our character. The accountant bears the imprint from decades of vouchers as surely as the carpenter bears the weight from tons of lumber and the jolt from thousands of hammer swings. The plumber's forearms are speckled with burns from molten solder, and the banker's face bears a crease for every foreclosure. Whatever else we make through our labor, we also make ourselves. So we had better choose carefully what we do with our days, and how we do it, and why.

&

The grunt of a diesel out front on Monday morning announces the arrival of the truck bearing our dumpster, a steel box large enough to hold most of a demolished house. When the driver takes a look at where I ask him to unload the dumpster, back down our narrow driveway hemmed in by limestone walls, he rubs his chin and says, "I don't know if it'll go."

It will, I tell him, because our neighbors, with whom we share the driveway, had a dumpster of the same size delivered from his company a year or so ago.

"Who was driving that time?" he asks me.

"Never caught his name," I answer. "Kind of a wiry guy, wore cowboy boots, hair slicked back."

"Well," says our driver, grabbing hold of the mirror mount and climbing back into his cab, "if he can do it, I can do it."

And he does, sawing the ungainly truck back and forth across our street, crushing piled snow with the fat rear wheels, finally easing back between the limestone walls with two or three inches of clearance on each side. He tilts the bed and lowers the dumpster, then nudges it backward until I give him a thumb's up. "How's that?" he shouts from his window.

"That's good driving," I shout back.

"You bet." He grins and waves as he drives off.

Soon after the truck rumbles away, Deryl shows up at the front door, fresh from an hour's reading of a new book on the origins of consciousness. He carries a tool belt in one hand, with a hammer dangling from the loop, and in the other hand a wrecking bar.

"Well, Scott," he says, "are you ready to tear up your house?"

"Ready as I'm going to be," I tell him.

Huffing and puffing through face masks, we light into the walls, knocking plaster loose in chunks that shatter on the floor, and we pry off the splintery laths. I think about the men who tacked those slender boards in place seventy years ago, who stirred horse hair into the mixture of lime and gypsum and sand to strengthen the plaster, and who spread the heavy mortar so evenly. Their work has held up well for three generations, and it would hold up for generations more, if we did not need to replace the rusted pipes and antiquated wiring and drafty window. When we tear out a false ceiling, the joists groan as they let go their grip on the nails. Every hour or so we pause in our demolition to shovel the debris down a chute into the dumpster.

During our breaks, Deryl stubbornly avoids smoking, since he is coddling his voice for an upcoming concert. Instead, he sips a cola and tells me about the book he's been reading, on the mysterious rise of consciousness, or he recites a verse from one of his new songs. Is that too sentimental? he asks me. No, I tell him, I like that verse just fine. Or he asks me if I think the human brain can be accounted for purely in evolutionary terms, seeing as how we have so much more thinking power than we need for survival, maybe a whole lot more than is good for us, like a teenager's jalopy with four hundred horsepower and poor brakes. As Deryl talks, one callused hand chisels his words into the air. The muscles of his arms bunch and leap under the taut skin. My own arms ache, and my hands lie wounded in my lap. Every summer the palms toughen up from rubbing against wood and steel and rock. But now, in late winter, after months of shuffling paper, they are as soft as old corduroy. For the next month or so, every time I drive a car, tap a keyboard, or hold a book, my fingers will grow numb from the swelling in my wrists.

৯

A generation or two ago it would have seemed less strange to relish hard work. My grandparents might smile at the laziness of Tom Sawyer, who fooled others into doing his chores, but they would remind you that Tom was a child. Grown-ups do their own chores, unless they are idlers, good-for-nothings, ne'er-do-wells. Grown-ups look after their own needs, provide for their families, help their neighbors, do something useful. So my grandparents taught by word and example. Any job worth doing is worth doing right, they used to say. The good laborer is worth his hire, they would say, quoting scripture, so do not bury your talent in the ground but use it in the world, for the master rewards his faithful servant. To try sliding by with the least effort, my grandparents believed, was to be guilty of a sin called sloth.

I knew this cluster of values by experience long before I heard it referred to as the work ethic, a phrase that has lost its edge from tumbling over the lips of too many cynical bosses and politicians. Whatever happened to the work ethic? laments the manager who wishes to squeeze more profit from his employees. Whatever happened to the work ethic? groans the official who wants to shrink the welfare rolls. As I understand it, a regard for the necessity and virtue of work has nothing to do with productivity or taxes, and everything to do with fulfilling one's humanity. As I have seen it embodied in the lives not only of grandparents but of parents and neighbors and friends, this ethic arises from a belief that the creation is a sacred gift, and that by working we express our gratitude and celebrate our powers. To honor that gift, we should live simply, honestly, conservingly, saving money and patching clothes and fixing what breaks, sharing what we have.

Those values are under assault every minute of the day in a consumer economy—from advertising, from the glittering goodies in stores, from the luxurious imagery of television, magazines, and films, and from a philosophy that views the universe not as a gift to be honored but as a warehouse to be ransacked. If money is meaning, if winning the lottery or beating the stock market defines success, if the goal of life is easy sensation, then why lift a finger so long as you can force someone or something else to do it for you?

I can think of many reasons to lift a finger, among them the delight in exercising skill, in sharing labor with companions, in planning a task and carrying it through, in bringing some benefit to the world. But the chief reason for relishing work is that it allows us to practice our faith, whatever that faith may be. The

Buddha advised his followers to seek right livelihood, to provide for their needs in a modest and responsible manner, with respect for other creatures, in harmony with the way of things. We show our understanding of the way of things by the quality of our work, whether or not we have heard the Buddha's teachings. The old theological debate as to whether salvation is to be gained by works or by faith begins from a false dichotomy. Faith concerns our sense of what is real, what is valuable, what is holy; work is how we act out that faith.

The Shakers condensed their faith into the maxim, "Hands to work, hearts to God." Anyone who has looked at their furniture or buildings can sense the clarity of their vision. "One feels that for the Shaker craftsmen," Thomas Merton observed, "love of God and love of truth in one's own work came to the same thing, and that work itself was a prayer, a communion with the inmost spiritual reality of things and so with God." Mother Ann Lee, who launched the Shaker movement, counseled her followers to "Do all your work as if you had a thousand years to live, and as you would if you knew you must die tomorrow."

If the purpose of life is not to acquire but to inquire, to seek understanding, to discover all we can about ourselves and the universe, to commune with the source of things, then we should care less about what we earn—money, prestige, salvation—and more about what we learn. In light of all we have to learn, the difference between dying tomorrow and a hundred years from tomorrow is not very great.

ॐ

Tomorrow, Deryl's partner, Steve Neuenschwander, will return from a week of studying the Mayan ruins in Mexico. I have met Steve, a man as clear as one of these late winter mornings after a thaw when the maple sap begins to rise; but I have not seen him work.

"He's an artist with a hammer and saw," Deryl tells me. "He makes me look like a wood butcher."

I doubt that anyone could make Deryl look like a wood butcher, his eyes and hands are so sure. But I know that Steve's arrival will fill up our small kitchen and put me out of a job.

In the evening, after Jesse comes home from school and soccer practice, he and I pry up the shabby linoleum and the buckled particle board underlayment that some quick-and-dirty remodeler installed back around the time of the first moon landing. We will replace it with plywood that should outlast us, and we will screw the plywood down instead of nailing it, to prepare a surface for the red oak flooring that will come to us from the hills of southern Indiana. Tonight we finish the breaking down; tomorrow we start the building up.

Before we go to bed, Jesse and I stand quietly in this room that has been whittled down to the bare studs and joists. It is the diagram of a house, a diagram carried in the minds of carpenters before it rose here on a foundation of limestone blocks. We can see on the two-by-fours where those vanished carpenters chalked their measurements. They measured well, plumbed and squared the walls, drove the nails home, as though they were building a shelter not for strangers but for sisters and brothers whom they would never meet.

THE WRITER
IN THE UNIVERSITY
ॐ

ANY WRITER WHO earns a living in a university is likely to grimace in recognition at the following anecdote, related by the poet Donald Hall: "When Roman Jakobson—great linguist, Harvard professor—was approached some years ago with the suggestion that Vladimir Nabokov might be appointed professor of Slavic, Jakobson was skeptical; he had nothing against elephants, he said, but he would not appoint one professor of zoology."

It is amusing to think of anyone, even the erudite Jakobson, condescending to Nabokov. And yet, after reading Nabokov's *Lectures on Literature*, compiled from the notes he used while teaching at Wellesley and Cornell, I suspect that his pedagogy would be disdained by most literary scholars today, for those lectures consist mainly of the reconstruction of plot and the appreciation of style. Nabokov had little use for the brands of criticism in vogue during his tenure in the academy (from 1941 until 1958, when the success of *Lolita* enabled him to stop teaching). "The study of the sociological or political impact of literature," he warned his classes, "has to be devised mainly for those who are by temperament or education immune to the aesthetic vibrancy of authentic literature, for those who do not experience the telltale tingle between the shoulder blades." He also warned them to avoid any psychological reading, especially that of "the Freudian denomination with its borrowed myths, shabby umbrellas, and dark backstairs." He dismissed Freud as "the Viennese witch doctor," and he never mentioned Marx. For all the notice he took of history, it might be the hubbub of hooligans in the street, irrelevant to art.

At the time Nabokov was delivering his lectures to the undergraduates of Wellesley and Cornell, it was still rare in this country for poets and novelists to become professors. There were a famous few, such as John Crowe Ransom, Allen Tate, Robert Penn Warren, and Yvor Winters; but even these few, as my list suggests, were usually known for their criticism and scholarship as well as for their fiction and poetry. Jean-Paul Sartre was exaggerating only slightly when he reported in 1947 that "nothing is more remote" from the American writer "than the idea of college or clerkship."

Since 1947, the idea of college and professorship has become quite a familiar one for American writers. Poets, novelists, playwrights, and essayists have crowded into universities from Atlantic to Pacific. No one has taken an exact census, but our numbers, I would guess, amount to a couple of thousand. We have entered the academy for reasons as diverse as our talents. Some of us relish teaching and the conversation about literature, while others merely grab our paychecks and rush back to our keyboards. Some are drawn to the university as the last sanctuary for books in a marginally literate culture. Some of us come here to escape loneliness. Others linger in the academy simply because, after eighteen or twenty years of schooling, we cannot imagine living anywhere else.

If we only taught what professors of literature have always taught, then our manifold presence in the university would have had little effect on the curriculum. But it seems that wherever two or three are gathered together in the name of poetry, there also shall be a program in creative writing. Again, no one knows the precise number, but there must be at least five hundred such programs, graduate or undergraduate, and the total steadily rises. John Barth, maestro of the fiction workshop at Johns Hopkins, has observed:

> Not economic recession, not declining literacy, failing bookstores, the usurpation of the kingdom of narrative by movies and television—nothing quenches the American thirst for courses in creative writing. In day school, night school, high school, college, graduate school, correspondence school, summer school, prison school; in writers' colonies and conferences and camps and cruises, it is scribble scribble scribble scribble scribble scribble scribble.

Rust Hills, fiction editor for *Esquire*, remarked a few years ago that "there can scarcely be an American writer in his thirties who hasn't been involved in a university writing program somewhere, some time in his life." And it seems that wherever a degree in creative writing is granted, there also shall be literary magazines, prizes, festivals, perhaps a series of poetry and short-story collections from the university press, and most likely a parade of visitors reading from their work.

This is something new under the sun. Training young writers and then employing them once they have received their degrees, sponsoring magazines that publish their work, often using their books in courses, the academy has become a patron of literature on a scale that makes the popes and Medicis look like pikers. Such a thriving enterprise needs no defense from me. Instead, I wish to voice a few misgivings. I wish to consider the dangers of our being on campuses in such large numbers—dangers for ourselves, for our students, and for literature.

Of course, nothing I say about this dramatic shift in the demography of writers can be read apart from the fact that I help swell the statistics. My department at Indiana University hired me fresh out of graduate school, thinking I would become a scholar;

but after I published one book of literary criticism and two dozen articles, my gray pachyderm skin showed through, revealing my true character as a maker of fictions. And so if I seem to be more alarmed than encouraged by the stampede of writers into the university, I never forget that I am one elephant in the herd.

ᚹ

The new alliance between literature and the academy has been troubling writers almost as long as it has been feeding them. Flannery O'Connor, one of the early stars to rise from a workshop (at the University of Iowa), was already fretting in the 1950s:

> In the last twenty years the colleges have been emphasizing creative writing to such an extent that you almost feel that any idiot with a nickel's worth of talent can emerge from a writing class able to write a competent story. In fact, so many people can now write competent stories that the short story as a medium is in danger of dying of competence. We want competence, but competence by itself is deadly. What is needed is the vision to go with it, and you do not get this from a writing class.

Denise Levertov, a frequent visitor on campuses, has voiced a similar concern about the fate of her own genre: "I detest the clever verse disguised as poetry that emanates so frequently from the academic poetry factories and makes its way so efficiently in the world, acclaimed by reviewers who, like the verse writers, suppose poetry to be a way of *manipulating* language."

O'Connor is not alone in worrying that Gresham's law might apply to literature as well as to economics—that bad currency will drive out good. And Levertov is not alone in reaching for an industrial metaphor when she hears the word *university*. In a scathing survey of contemporary fiction, for example, William Gass laments that "in the Detroits of our culture, the manufacture of writers continues":

You may have noticed the plague of school-styled poets with which our pages have been afflicted, and taken some account of the no-account magazines that exist in order to publish them. In addition, thousands of short-story readers and writers have been released like fingerlings into the thin mainstream of serious prose.

In "Poetry and Ambition," the essay from which I quoted the anecdote about Nabokov and Jakobson, Donald Hall likens writing classes to sweatshops, assembly lines, and fastfood franchises. "The weekly meetings of the workshop serve the haste of our culture," forcing apprentice writers to churn out manuscript by the pound, mass-producing bland verse, which Hall refers to, unlovingly, as McPoems. Literary fads sweep through workshops the way hair styles sweep through teenage gangs. Students feel a compulsion to be up-to-date, as do many of their instructors, not suspecting that much of this year's modish fiction and poetry will be featured in next year's Salvation Army book sale.

Even such an accomplished teacher as Richard Hugo, a vigorous defender of classes in creative writing, attributes their popularity at least in part to "the narcissism of students, the egocentric disregard of knowledge, the laziness, the easy good grades to be had in the writing courses." "Here," according to William Gass, "many hide from academic requirements and from intellectual challenge. There are always shining exceptions, of course, but on the whole the students show little interest in literature. They are interested in writing instead . . . expressing a self as shallow as a saucer." I find that judgment too harsh, yet there is enough truth in it to provoke a fretful nod from anyone who has read a few thousand student manuscripts. Narcissism and anti-intellectualism afflict not only students but also many teachers and curricula, as Eve Shelnutt argues in a searching essay that carries its thesis in the title: "Notes from a Cell: Creative Writing Programs in Isolation."

While I find more shining exceptions among student writers than Gass would seem to, I share his worries about the training we offer them. Consider what it means, for example, that MFA programs in creative writing hardly ever require knowledge of foreign languages. How can one think responsibly about life in our time or discover the full potential of literature without a lively interest in other cultures? In this last decade of the millennium, more than ever in history, our sympathies and reading need to be global, not limited to work in English, let alone to recent American writing.

For a sample of global awareness, look at *Six Memos for the Next Millennium*, the series of lectures that Italo Calvino was preparing just before his death. There you will find quotations ranging over three thousand years of literature, in Latin, German, Spanish, French, and English, as well as in his native Italian. Or look at the multi-lingual, multi-disciplinary references in Milan Kundera's *Art of the Novel*, or the international perspective in Nadine Gordimer's *Essential Gesture*. Reading Gordimer, Kundera, or Calvino, one encounters a mind fully adequate to our age and condition. By ignoring languages and history, by slighting the study of literature from earlier centuries, by excluding from the workshop disciplines like philosophy and science, the curricula of many writing programs enforce a parochialism that has nothing to do with the address of the university.

ૐ

Robert Penn Warren attributed much of his own sense of craft to his experience as a teacher of great literature. Such teaching is no longer typical for writers, who are often expected—and often desire—to conduct workshops exclusively. Instead of reading the major works of our predecessors and contemporaries, we read stacks of apprentice work. "The poet," Donald Hall cautions, "may prolong adolescence into retirement by dealing only with the products of infant brains." Although Theodore Roethke composed eloquent apologies for the teaching of creative writing, he also gave vent to this tirade:

> Lord, I'm plumb tuckered out lugging these hunks of pork up the lower slopes of Parnassus, knowing all the time that as soon as I turn around, back they'll slip to blurbanity, inanity, and the dearest, dullest people in the world. I'm tired of being a day-laborer on this canary-farm, a ladies' maid in a seminary of small beasts, a mid-wife sweating to effect a most particular parturition: bringing forth little maimed ends of life, poems with all the charm (if they don't lay eggs) of aborted salamanders.

"I ask you," Roethke concludes, "is that the way for a grown man, and me past thirty-five, to make a living?"

We are not supposed to admit feeling such resentment, such exasperation. But what teaching writer, at least every now and again, has not felt so? Frank O'Connor explains that he quit his job at Harvard because, after helping students improve their fiction, he had neither time nor energy for his own. "I don't believe in teaching poetry at all," Elizabeth Bishop told an interviewer, "but that's what they want one to do. You see so many poems every week, you just lose all sense of judgment." It is odd, when you think about it, that an Elizabeth Bishop, a Frank O'Connor, or a Theodore Roethke, in his or her prime, should have to earn a living by coaching beginners instead of by writing.

As teachers, we must describe analytically what, as artists, we do instinctively. Surrounded by colleagues who are scholars and critics, we may be tempted to write for that specialized audience; our experience of the world may be cramped; our ears may lose the sound of unfettered speech. The ethos of the academy is aloof, rational, dispassionate. Insofar as writers take on these attitudes, their art is likely to suffer. On the other hand, if writers violate the decorum of the academy—as the remarks I have quoted from Barth, Gass, and Roethke do—they may be dismissed as hotheads or curmudgeons. And yet, without passion, without an openness to the unconscious, without a willingness to appear ignorant or foolish or rude, without omnivorous curiosity, without a sympathy for the full human range, the writer is doomed to superficiality. Denise Levertov has cautioned that "teaching, even at its most rewarding, uses up some of the same kind of energies that go into [one's] own work; therefore I think it is extremely risky for any artist to teach full-time—perhaps especially if he enjoys teaching." If life in the university is risky for the individual poet or novelist, it can be disastrous for literature when it becomes the one way of life common to a generation of writers. A teaching position can be a kind of exile if the writer only ventures off campus to give readings or attend conferences at other schools. I am reminded of George Orwell's warning about the dangers of geographical exile: "Exile is probably more damaging to a novelist than to a painter or even a poet, because its effect is to take him out of contact with working life and narrow down his range to the street, the café, the church, the brothel and the studio." In much of the writing that has emerged from universities, the range of reference is even more constricted: the brothel is replaced by the motel, the studio by the study, the church by the shopping mall, and the life of streets by the stream of consciousness.

E. L. Doctorow, himself a professor, has complained that "the horizon of the university-trained writers is diminished; the field for their work and attention is generally the bedroom, the living room, the family. The doors are closed, the shades are pulled down, and it's as if there were no streets outside, and no town, no highway, no society."

Since I quoted Flannery O'Connor's misgivings about the boom in creative writing, it is only fair that I quote her defense against charges like Doctorow's:

> We hear a great deal of lamentation these days about writers having all taken themselves to the colleges and universities where they live decorously instead of going out and getting firsthand information

about life. The fact is that anybody who has survived his childhood has enough information about life to last him the rest of his days. If you can't make something out of a little experience, you probably won't be able to make it out of a lot. The writer's business is to contemplate experience, not to be merged in it.

Insofar as this is an argument against the he-man school of writing epitomized by Hemingway, I agree with it. And I also agree with O'Connor's Jamesian insistence that our task is not to collect experiences like trophies but, rather, to be one on whom no experience—no matter how circumscribed—is lost. But I disagree with her celebrated claim that childhood provides us with enough information to last us the rest of our days. A literature that limits itself to the trials and tribulations of growing up will never be grown up. After completing her degree, O'Connor herself left the university and returned to the farm, the countryside, and the small towns that furnished the materials for her stories. When she wrote about children, she viewed them through the eyes of an adult, one who knew intimately the language, the labors, and the outlook of her Georgia neighbors.

As a higher and higher proportion of our writers learn their craft and make their living in the academy, often with no break between gaining their degrees and joining a faculty, it is inevitable that our literature will embody a narrower range of settings, occupations, and social classes. One might apply Orwell's own metaphor and speak of the university not as an ivory tower but as a whale, with the writer a Jonah snug inside: "The whale's belly is simply a womb big enough for an adult. There you are, in the dark, cushioned space that exactly fits you, with yards of blubber be-tween yourself and reality, able to keep up an attitude of the completest indifference, no matter *what* happens." The security of a teaching position makes it easier for the writer to adopt a stance of cultivated despair, to indulge in verbal games, or to wear an insulating layer of irony. Such coyness and posturing, however sophisticated they may seem in the individual writer, would, if multiplied a thousandfold, be a plague on literature.

≥

The university has become a still more hazardous home for writers because of the Great Awakening now spreading from campus to campus under the banner of Theory. Even in the most convivial of times, a degree of hostility between writers and critics—as between rival soccer teams—may be inevitable. After studying criticism under John Crowe Ransom at Kenyon, E. L. Doctorow felt the need to unlearn those habits of mind before he could once again make fiction: "So all in all as valuable as my training was, it took me through language in the wrong direction. It cost me a few years of writing time to recover my ignorance, the way I felt about writing as a child." Criticism deals in abstractions, literature in the concrete; criticism aims at analysis, literature at synthesis. Critics usually prefer their authors to be safely dead and, therefore, incapable of springing surprises, while authors prefer to be alive and unpredictable.

Even in convivial times, as I said, these two parties might glare at one another from opposite benches. And these are not convivial times. Here, for example, is John Gardner's assessment of recent developments:

No depressed and angry writer at the present moment can fail to notice, if he raises his weary head and looks around, that fools, maniacs, and jabberers are everywhere—mindless, tasteless, ignorant schools of criticism publishing fat journals and meeting in solemn conclave, completely misreading great writers, or celebrating tawdry imitation writers to whom not even a common farm duck would give his ear; other schools maintain, with much talk of Heidegger, that nothing a writer writes means anything, the very existence of his page is an amusing accident, all the words are a lunatic blithering (for all the writer's care), since language is by nature false and misleading.

[107]

Again, Gardner violates the decorum of the academy. Scholars do not describe those with whom they disagree as maniacs, nor do they compare them unfavorably with ducks. As a student of the Middle Ages, Gardner could hold his own at flyting. Even discounted for his love of high dudgeon, such a passage conveys the unease that many writers feel in the face of what Terry Eagleton has called "a really virulent outbreak of theory, on an epidemic scale."

Toni Morrison responds to the newly hostile climate in more sober terms:

> Writers are less and less central to the idea and subject of literature. Whole schools of criticism have dispossessed the writer of any place whatever in the critical value of his work. Ideas, craft, vision, meaning—all of them are just so much baggage in these critical systems. The text itself is a mere point of departure for philology, philosophy, psychiatry, theology and other disciplines. The political consequences for minority writers, dissident writers and writers committed to social change are devastating. For it means that there is no way to talk about what we mean, because to mean anything is not in vogue.

Rightly or wrongly, many of us who make stories and poems feel that the net effect of recent theorizing has been to turn the writer into a puppet, one whose strings are jerked by some higher power—by ideology or the unconscious, by genetics, by ethnic allegiance, by sexual proclivities, by gender, by language itself. We may wade through Derrida and Adorno and de Man, we may read Harold Bloom and J. Hillis Miller and Stanley Fish, or we may simply hear rumors of what they and their followers are up to; whether at first- or secondhand, we learn that to regard ourselves as conscious, purposeful, responsible artists is a delusion; we learn that material conditions or neuroses control us; we learn that our efforts at making sense are doomed to failure; we learn that our words, like Zeno's forlorn rabbit, will never reach their destination. We see that a new priesthood has arisen, adepts who must intervene between reader and book, between the benighted commoner and elusive Meaning.

Not only writers view the current atmosphere of literary studies in this bleak light. Consider, for example, this reading by the British critic Patrick Parrinder:

> To judge by a good deal of recent writing, the following resolutions would attract majority support at a conference of devotees of literary theory:
>
> 1. We are living at a time of "theoretical revolution" in the humanities.
> 2. The theorist is no longer a servant of the literary critic. Theory and criticism should not take second place to imaginative writing.
> 3. All utterances are implicitly theoretical. All theory is political. The task of the theorist is to uncover, and where necessary to denounce, the theoretical-political implications of all discourse whatever.
> 4. The enemies of theory are politically conservative. Theory is radical, and so are its advocates. Pragmatists are not to be trusted.
> 5. 'Literature' is now a redundant category. The study of English literature is in a terminal state and ought to wither away.
> 6. English lecturers, however, ought not to be made redundant.
> 7. There is not much to be learnt from contemporary novelists, dramatists and poets. The author is dead. Long live the Theorist!

Of course the death of the author is not a slogan calculated to please a living one; of course we would prefer not to think of ourselves as puppets. Accordingly, our unease may be dismissed as self-serving, indeed as evidence in support of those theories that are premised on a belief in our naiveté.

Perhaps we are only receiving our due after having long abused the critics. Witness Ezra Pound, that failed professor: "Pay no attention to the criticism of men who have never themselves written a notable work." Or Jean-Paul Sartre: "The critic lives badly; his wife does not appreciate him as she ought to; his children are ungrateful; the first of the month is hard on him." Or William Faulkner: "The artist doesn't have time to listen to the critics. . . . The artist is a cut above the critic, for the artist is writing something which will move the critic. The critic is writing something which will move everybody but the artist." Or John Cheever, who observes maliciously:

> The vast academic world exists like everything else, on what it can produce that will secure an income. So we have papers on fiction, but they come out of what is largely an industry. In no way does it help those who write fiction or those who love to read fiction. The whole business is a subsidiary undertaking, like extracting useful chemicals from smoke.

Thus the industrial metaphor shows up again, used here for lambasting critics.

Contemporary theory has inverted Faulkner's hierarchy, elevating the critic above the artist. The resulting condescension can be reminiscent of Victorian anthropology: instead of benighted savages, bound by ignorance and superstition, we now have benighted authors. Writing students often bump into this attitude in graduate seminars, where they are mocked for confessing that they have been moved by a work or for considering the truth of a literary vision. Unlike Nabokov, teachers of seminars are rarely interested in whether or not literature provokes a tingle between the shoulder blades. As a result, young writers do sometimes feel like elephants, basking in sunshine and munching hay, scorned by the learned zoologists.

Poets and novelists, who spend their days worrying about words, may be repelled by critical theory simply because much of it is abominably written. On this point, I favor the judgment offered by Primo Levi, who brought to the writing of prose a scientist's regard for precision and clarity:

> He who does not know how to communicate, or communicates badly, in a code that belongs only to him or a few others, is unhappy, and spreads unhappiness around him. If he communicates badly deliberately, he is wicked or at least a discourteous person, because he imposes labor, anguish, or boredom on his readers.

The making of a poem or novel is an act of inclusion, a drawing in of readers to share an experience; too often, the making of literary theory is an act of exclusion, shutting out all but the cognoscenti. Writers may ignore theory because they find little there that serves their art or their understanding of the world. They may pass over deconstructionism or new historicism because they are too busy keeping up with particle physics, say, or liberation theology, with plate tectonics or Mayan ethnography.

While at work on this essay, I read *The Company We Keep* by Wayne Booth, *Protocols of Reading* by Robert Scholes, and *The Call of Stories* by Robert Coles, all of which go to great lengths to argue that writing has an ethical and political dimension; that readers are not merely playing among signs but are taking in and comparing visions of what it means to be human; that literature informs the conduct of life. It is a worrisome reflection on the state of criticism when three such prominent figures feel the need to make that case. To suggest how writers themselves have made the same case—about the links between writing and living—I can do no more within the bounds of this essay than point to the works by Calvino, Kundera, and Gordimer already mentioned, or to these five spirited books: Gary Synder's *The Real Work*, Annie Dillard's *Living by Fiction*, Wendell Berry's *Standing by Words*, Ursula Le Guin's *Dancing at the Edge of the World*, and Salman Rushdie's *Imaginary Homelands*.

Even if this were the place, I would not be the person to take on literary theory in all its variety and complexity. But let me at least mention some of the points that trouble me. I believe that the extreme forms of subjectivist or reader-response theories, by granting the reader total power of interpretation, elevate solipsism into a critical principle and make nonsense of the writer's concern for craft. As Robert Scholes has mildly observed, "Reading comes after writing. We must look backward and find something there in order to be reading at all." Debates about the canon that focus entirely on sociological criteria have the effect of devaluing artistic criteria, the only ones over which the writer has any control, since he or she cannot change gender, ethnic identity, or class. Although writers cannot of course know all the forces that impinge on them, nor can they achieve all that they intend, their knowledge and their intentions have more bearing on their art than the deconstructionists would allow. Any theory that treats the critic as an autonomous intellect while treating the writer as an ignorant captive—of class, language, or gender—is a fraud. The death of the author has been too dearly purchased if it serves merely as a condition for the rebirth of the critic.

ᏱᎯ

As a writer and a professor, I live with an acute awareness of all these dangers: that literature may shrivel in an arena of hostile theories; that deep and original work may be lost in a flood of the merely competent; that self-indulgence may be mistaken for creativity, ignorance for inspiration; that talking about art may become a substitute for making it.

After this gloomy recital, I feel the need to say—as Mark Twain said of Wagner's music—that it's not as bad as it sounds. No doubt there are many literary scholars, including some theorists, who would agree with Wayne Booth that "the most important of all critical tasks is to participate in—and thus to reinforce—a critical culture, a vigorous conversation, that will nourish in return those who feed us with narratives." Writers may continue to find a home in the academy so long as a few of their colleagues think of narratives as food, not fodder.

Of course, good writers can be poor teachers. They may be lazy, selfish, dumb. They may be cynical careerists. They may never unpack their suitcases, waiting for better offers. They may subscribe to William Styron's opinion that the "professor should weed out the good from the bad, cull them like a farmer, and not encourage the ones who haven't got something." They may embrace the romantic view of the artist as a genius to whom the world's demands are an inconvenience, if not an insult. And yet the blessed fact remains that some distinguished writers have also been distinguished teachers. Think of Wallace Stegner at Stanford, Richard Hugo at Montana, Grace Paley at Sarah Lawrence, William Stafford at Lewis and Clark. For all their skepticism about the teaching of creative writing, John Barth, John Gardner, and Theodore Roethke have, according to their former students, done it surpassingly well. Gardner's influence, for example, has been celebrated by Raymond Carver, Charles Johnson, and Nicholas Delbanco, all of whom became worthy teachers and writers in their turn.

Of course, most of the thousands of students currently enrolled in creative writing programs will never publish anything of note. The same could be said of students in any field. And yet each year some writers of considerable talent do graduate, if only because they were talented to begin with. For all students, regardless of talent, and for faculty members as well, the university can serve as a substitute for the café, the salon, the literary circle. Writers have always sought out one another's company. So they gather in the Lake District; in London; in the south of France; in Buenos Aires; in Concord, Massachusetts; in Greenwich Village. What the workshop ideally provides is a community of people who read widely and well, who savor words, who enjoy using their minds, who take seriously what young writers wish to take seriously. Such a community is all the more vital in a society where books in general and literature in particular have been shoved to the margin, where language has been debased, where the making of art seems foolish beside the making of money.

On a visit to the workshop at Columbia University, Jorge Luis Borges said that what apprentices need more than anything else is friendship and literary conversation: "We owe all young writers the opportunity of getting together, of agreeing or disagreeing, and finally of achieving the craft of writing." Craft certainly can be taught, even if genius cannot. "Art is the habit of the artist," Flannery O'Connor insists, "and habits have to be rooted deep in the whole personality. They have to be cultivated like any other habit, over a long period of time, by experience; and teaching any kind of writing is largely a matter of helping the student develop the habit of art." Perhaps we cannot teach curiosity or sensitivity or insight, but we can honor those gifts when we find them. To his audience of aspiring writers, Borges said, "Every young poet thinks of himself as Adam, naming things. The truth is that he is not Adam and that he has a long tradition behind him. That tradition is the language he is writing in and the literature he has read." Something of this rich inheritance can also be taught. If we do our jobs well, we can persuade young writers to feel, as Pound maintains, that the "tradition is a beauty which we preserve and not a set of fetters to bind us."

However often we may be told by our colleagues that literature is really about the processes of art, readers outside the academy still expect literature to be about the world. "People like the world," says Annie Dillard.

> Many people actually prefer it to art and spend their days by choice in the thick of it. . . . When the arts abandon the world as their subject matter, people abandon the arts. And when wide audiences abandon the arts, the arts are free to pursue whatever theories led them to abandon the world in the first place. They are as free as wandering albatrosses or stamp collectors or technical rock climbers; no one is looking.

If we expect readers to keep looking our way, we will need to lift our eyes and gaze about. Language is not a prison house; on the contrary, it is the means of our freedom. With Calvino, we should celebrate "the use of words as . . . a perpetual pursuit of things, as a perpetual adjustment to their infinite variety." Language arises from our shared life, and, for all its imprecision, points to everything we are capable of sharing.

I could imagine a program in writing fashioned along the lines proposed by Gary Snyder: "Now if I were teaching a poetry course at the university and I had everything I needed, there would have to be a sauna right there, and a quarter of an acre of garden plot, and a good kitchen, and some musical instruments and God knows what-all." If I had comparable freedom, I would take my classes on field trips to forests and rivers and caves, to museums, to warehouses and factories, to quarries and mines, to housing projects and trailer parks, to chemistry labs and cyclotrons, to playgrounds and barbershops. I would urge my students to learn a trade—farming or carpentry, welding or weaving, cooking or sewing or surveying. Study the soils, I would say, learn the plants and animals, walk the streets, listen to the rhythms of your place and the voices of your neighbors. Settle somewhere. And if that somewhere happens to be a university, I would tell them, don't mistake it for the universe.

NEWS OF THE WILD

ॐ

MY DAUGHTER EVA and I are preparing for a trip into the Boundary Waters of northern Minnesota. This will be my first long canoe journey since the death of my father, who taught me how to paddle, and for Eva it will be the first ever. As I work through the checklist of items to pack, I find myself wondering how I let her reach the age of twenty without our having taken such a trip before. I could easily blame circumstances, the demands of work and family, the cost. But the deeper source of my delay, I realize, has been a worry that I cannot be as true a guide for Eva in wild places as my father was for me.

Although he spent his working years in factories and offices, when I think of my father I see him outdoors. Whether in a garden, pasture, or woods, on a river or lake, he was always looking around, sniffing the air, listening, and he always seemed utterly at ease. "Happy as a hog in corn," he used to say. Mosquitoes would not bite him, bees would not sting him, poison ivy would not cause him the least itch. Bucking horses gentled under his hand, barking dogs lowered their hackles when he spoke, surly bears and gluttonous raccoons padded away after exchanging stares with him, and snakes kept clear of his feet. If wildness ever frightened him—

including the wildness of a quirky heart that would eventually kill him—he never let on.

His favorite excuse for leaving the house was the old and respectable one of fishing. He took me first to dangle hooks in ponds, then in reservoirs, then farther and farther afield, beyond the scruffy edges of towns, beyond roofs and roads and utility wires, until we came at last into country where the human signs were too faint for us to see. "Looks like God just now closed up the toolbox and finished work on this place," he told me once on an island in Ontario's Algonquin Park. No matter how wild or tame the place, he seemed equally at home. He never complained of being tired or sore, hot or hungry or cold. He would as soon camp beside a spillway as beside a waterfall. He inspected pebbles with the same attention he gave to mountains. If we caught fish, fine; if not, that also was fine.

These outings were never trials of endurance, with a quota of miles to cover and hazards to overcome, but always musing saunters. "Will you look at this," he would say, and time and again we paused to look. Paddling through rapids, portaging between moosey lakes, hunting for arrowheads in a plowed field, or picking beans in the yard, he moved with the same deliberation and delight. The point was to be in contact with dirt and water and wood and sky, in the presence of animals, wide awake. Whatever his indoor faults, and he certainly had them, when he was outdoors my father radiated a steady, savoring attentiveness, and that was a great gift. He was so mindful of the Creation that in his company I forgot clocks and calendars, let go of words, and became mindful as well.

Remembering him as I pack for the canoe trip, I realize that I must add tobacco to my checklist. Eva raises her eyebrows at this. I explain to her that the Ojibwa, through whose country we will paddle, sprinkled tobacco on the water before setting out in a canoe, as an offering to the spirits for a safe journey. Unless honored in this way, the Water Monster might devour you or

Thunderbirds might drown you. When I first learned of this practice and told my father, he said that sounded like a mighty sensible idea, as sensible as the design for canoes, moccasins, and domed wigwam tents we borrowed from the Great Lakes tribes. After that, every time he and I traveled by water, he would hand me one of his cigarettes, and I would tear it open and scatter the brown shreds on the waves.

This awkward ceremony gave me a hint of the dignity that tobacco still possessed for a people who used it only in solemn dealings with one another and in speaking with the gods. Just as we have stripped the holiness from tobacco with our incessant smoking, so we have stripped the holiness from travel with our commuting, our tourism, our idle shuttling about. When America was all wilderness except for occasional villages and orchards and cleared fields, a journey of any distance was a serious undertaking, whatever your ancestry, for there was always a good chance you would become lost, be captured by enemies, be injured, or die. Knowing the dangers, you prepared yourself with song and sacred tales and prayers. Traveling through forest or desert, over prairies, along rivers, you could never forget that your life depended on the wild web of creatures and forces, nor could you forget how vanishingly small a knot you were in that great web.

If you belonged to the Ojibwa or some other rooted people, when you returned from a long and perilous journey, your family and neighbors would ask if you had learned a new song, met a new animal, come upon a healing herb or a source of food or a holy place. What vision had you brought back for the community? The prime reason for traveling, after all, was to enrich the life at home.

"What did you find?" my father would ask when I returned from a camping trip or an after-dinner stroll. And I would show him a fossil or feather, tell him how sun lit up the leaves of a hickory, how a skunk looked me over; I would recall for him the taste of elderberries or the rush of wind in white pines or the crunch of locust shells underfoot. Only in that sharing of what I had found was the journey completed, the circle closed.

I have put some version of my father's question to both of my children, my son Jesse as well as Eva, from the time they could toddle. What did you find? What did you see? What's out there? I ask not merely because my father did, nor in paleskin imitation of the native people, but because I want to know the answer. I want to know what is out there, for my children, for me, for all of us. I want to bring what is out there in here, inside the walls where I live most of my hours, inside my porous and temporary skin, into the tumbling river of my thoughts, into my soul. By speaking of soul, a word worn slick from rolling over too many tongues, I wish to name that within me which rises up in response to the power and beauty I meet in the world. Whether we are bound through our depths to anything eternal, I cannot say; but I am certain we are bound, through and through, to all of nature. Our dependence on the great web is easier to see in the backwoods, but it is no less true in the backyard. Bringing home news from the wild is only a way of acknowledging that the wild is always and inescapably our home.

If I can help Eva to feel that, I will have passed on to her something of my father's gift to me. Talking of what we hope to see, she and I begin our journey long before we dip our paddles in the water, before we load the canoe, before we lace our boots, and the journey will continue after we have taken our seats once more beside the kitchen table. At the beginning we will say a prayer or two, and at the end, if we keep ourselves open and if the spirits bless us, we will bring back a few good stories. We will carry a pouch of tobacco to placate the old water monsters, along with a water-treatment kit to placate the new ones, those poisons and parasites we two-leggeds have flushed into the remotest rivers and lakes. We will also take bottles of sunscreen to compensate for the tattering of the ozone screen. There is no getting beyond the human reach, even in the Boundary Waters, just as there is no getting beyond the sway of earth, not without a spaceship.

The criterion for deciding what to load in a canoe or backpack is the same as that for deciding what to load in a spaceship: Is it worth its weight? Eva and I have winnowed down our gear and food to an amount we can carry. What we portage across land and paddle across water is only a tiny portion of what we need, of course. To provide everything we need, we would have to carry the sun and moon and stars, fruitful grass, fertile soil, nourishing sea, trees and ferns, bacteria and bears, rock and rain and air, and the countless moorings of our love. No pack smaller than the universe would hold it all.

VOYAGEURS

for Olivia Ladd Gilliam

IN MORNING MIST on a northern river, a slab of stone tumbled from a boulder into the water, where it came to life and floated, turning into a sleek black head that swam in circles dragging a V of ripples behind it. A beaver, I thought, as I watched from shore. But no sooner had I named it than the creature bobbed up and then dove, exposing a long neck and humped back and pointed tail. Not a beaver, I realized, but an otter. I was pleased to find a label for this animate scrap, as though by pinning the right word on the shape-shifter I could hold it still.

Presently a second otter, then a third and fourth broke free of the boulder and slithered down into the mercury sheen of the river. They dove without a splash, their tails flipping up to gleam like wands in the early sunlight, and they surfaced so buoyantly that their forepaws and narrow shoulders lifted well out of the water. Then one after another they clambered back onto the rock and dove again, over and over, like tireless children taking turns on a playground slide.

My daughter Eva came to stand beside me, the hood of her parka drawn up against the cool of this July morning here in the north woods, on the boundary between Minnesota and Ontario.

We passed her binoculars back and forth, marveling at these sleek, exuberant animals.

"Wouldn't you love to swim with them?" she whispered.

"I'd love to sit on that boulder and let them do the swimming," I answered.

"If only they'd let us!"

Always quick to notice the flicker of life, Eva had spent the past two summers studying birds with a research team, and now, halfway through college, she had become a disciplined as well as a passionate observer. Science had complicated her vision without lessening her delight in other creatures.

"What do you suppose they're doing?" I asked.

"The technical term for it," she said, "is goofing around."

"I suppose you've got some data to back that up."

"I'll show you the graphs when we get home."

Drawn by our whispers and watchfulness, the others from our camp soon joined us on the granite bluff, some bearing mugs of coffee, some with plates of steaming blueberry pancakes. We had been canoeing in the Boundary Waters Wilderness for several days, long enough for the men's faces to stubble with beards, for the women's faces to burnish from wind and sun. When all ten of us were gathered there beside the river, intently watching, suddenly the otters quit diving, swiveled their snouts in our direction, then ducked into hiding beneath some lily pads. After a couple of minutes, as though having mulled over what to do about this intrusion, they sallied out again and resumed their romping, chasing one another, bobbing and plunging, but farther and farther away, until they disappeared around the next bend.

If our scent or voices had not spooked them, then our upright silhouettes, breaking the glacier-smoothed outline of the shore, must have signaled danger to the otters. There was no way of knowing what else, if anything, we meant to them. What did the otters mean to us? What held us there while our pancakes cooled, while acres of mist rode the current past our feet, while the sun rose above a jagged fringe of trees and poured creamy light onto the river? What did we want from these elegant swimmers?

Or, to put the question in the only form I can hope to answer, what did *I* want? Not their hides, as the native people of this territory, the Ojibwa, or the old French voyageurs might have wanted; not their souls or meat. I did not even want their photograph, although I found them surpassingly beautiful. I wanted their company. I desired their instruction—as if, by watching them, I might learn to belong somewhere as they so thoroughly belonged here. I yearned to slip out of my skin and into theirs, to feel the world for a spell through their senses, to think otter thoughts, and then to slide back into myself, a bit wiser for the journey.

In tales of shamans the world over, men and women make just such leaps, into hawks or snakes or bears, and then back into human shape, their vision enlarged, their sympathy deepened. I am a poor sort of shaman. My shape never changes, except, year by year, to wrinkle and sag. I did not become an otter, even for an instant. But the yearning to leap across the distance, the reaching out in imagination to a fellow creature, seems to me a worthy impulse, perhaps the most encouraging and distinctive one we have. It is the same impulse that moves us to reach out to one another across differences of race or gender, age or class. What I desired from the otters was also what I most wanted from my daughter and from the friends with whom we were canoeing, and it is what I have always desired from neighbors and strangers. I wanted their blessing. I wanted to dwell alongside them with understanding and grace. I wanted them to go about their lives in my presence as though I were kin to them, no matter how much I might differ from them outwardly.

&

The root of *wild* means shaggy hair, and *wilderness* means an unruly place where shaggy creatures roam. I became shaggier during our stay in the Boundary Waters, for I had left my razor at home in Indiana, as I had left behind my watch, calendar, and books. Because of limited cargo space in the canoes, and because every item would have to be portaged many times, each of us was allotted for personal gear a bag the size of a grocery sack. Packing for the trip, Eva and I whittled away and whittled away, aiming to carry only the essentials.

Discovering the essentials, after all, is reason enough for going to the wilderness. When everything that you will use for a week must ride on your back or on the back of a friend, you think hard about what you truly need. With twice the cargo space, I still would not have carried a calendar or a watch, not even a book, my favorite tool. I wished to unplug myself from all our ingenious grids; to withdraw from print, from telephones, mailboxes, computers, from radio and television. There were the earth and sky to read, sun and belly for keeping time. As for the razor, my whiskers would grow without any tending.

I decided not to shave on the morning of our departure. By the next morning, when we reached our putting-in spot on Fall Lake, near Ely, Minnesota, I looked like a bum, according to Eva.

"If you wrapped yourself in a greasy blanket," she told me, "you could beg for spare change."

I rasped a palm along my jaw, but I would not see the bristles until my return home, for I avoided mirrors in truck stop restrooms on the drive to and from the Boundary Waters. As we slid our canoes into Fall Lake shortly after dawn, the surface was calm enough to mirror the shore, and I could have studied my reflection by gazing straight down. Yet I felt no desire to see my face, not then, not once all week. I meant to leave behind whatever I could that had the word *my* attached to it.

On that first day, Eva and I paddled together, she in the bow and I in the stern. We were out of practice, and so, while the other four canoes in our party pulled straight across the water, we traced a zigzag path. As the day wore on, however, and we wore down, shoulders beginning to ache, we stopped trying so hard and eventually found our rhythm. For minutes at a stretch, I forgot the canoe, forgot myself. Breathing and paddling and seeing became a single motion, a gliding meditation. Then a rock would loom before us, a gust of wind would jostle us, a hawk would call or a muscle twitch, and suddenly I would be yanked back into myself. There were my hands gripping the paddle, there were the boxy green packs leaning together over the middle thwart, there was Eva with ponytail swaying beneath her plum-colored hat, there was the gulf once more between seer and seen.

What I saw hemming the water on all sides was a low-slung terrain that had been scoured down to bedrock by glaciers, had been thronged with pine and spruce and aspen and birch over the next ten thousand years, had been stripped again to bedrock by loggers, and was now being slowly reclaimed by forest. Here and there the spiky green humps of islands broke through the gray plane of water. On the portages between lakes, staggering beneath the weight of canoes or rucksacks over trails worn down through mud and roots to stone, we could see how thin the soil was, how precarious the hold of life.

After one of those portages, as we started the long pull down Pipestone Bay, the wind picked up and blew somber clouds from the north. We could see the rain coming, like a translucent scrim wafting toward us over the water. By the time Eva and I put on our slickers, the squall had blown past, and we found ourselves sweating in sunlight. So we peeled off the slickers, only to see another curtain of rain approaching, and behind it another dose of sun. After three or four cloudbursts, wet from without and within, we gave up on rain gear and paddled on through whatever the sky delivered.

"How're you doing?" I asked Eva during a lull between showers.

"So far so good," she answered. "Those years of ballet may have messed up my feet, but they've given me stamina."

"You're not chilled, are you?"

"I'm fine, Daddy."

"Maybe take some extra vitamin C tonight."

From the bow came a sigh, then silence. At twenty, Eva was the youngest in our group, and I was the oldest at forty-seven. She was the only one who had a parent along, a fact that annoyed her whenever I reminded her of it by some fatherly gesture. She was also annoyed when any of our companions seemed to coddle her—by urging her to carry a lighter pack on the portages, for example, or by offering her the first food at a meal.

I have called those companions friends, because that is what they became by journey's end; but at the beginning I scarcely knew these four women and four men. Our friendship came about less through the sharing of a landscape than through the sharing of good work. From dawn until dusk, we lifted, carried, paddled, hiked, packed and unpacked, sawed, cooked, and scrubbed. The work was good because every bit of it served an obvious need—to move, to eat, to shelter, to keep warm—and because all of us joined in willingly, taking up whatever job was there to be done, helping one another without being asked. Only when the chores were finished did we swim or sing or pick berries or stretch out on sun-warmed stone and talk.

We camped that first night within earshot of Basswood Falls, and as I lay in the tent, the thrum of water made me feel as though I were still afloat. Waiting for sleep, I heard from muscles and joints I had not thought of for a long time.

❧

I woke in darkness to the wacky sound of loons, a pair of them wailing back and forth like two blues singers demented by love. Listening, I felt the tug of desires I could not name.

Before setting out again, we changed canoeing partners. I knew that Eva would be glad not to have me looking over her shoulder as we paddled. Out from under my gaze, her own gaze grew keener. She was the first to spy a bald eagle perched on a dead tree, as she was the first to spy blueberries and raspberries on our portages, the first to notice the swoop of a peregrine falcon and the pale blue sprays of harebells on shoreline rocks. Since her birth, she had been restoring to me lost pieces of the world or disclosing pieces I had never known.

From its perch the eagle followed our slow progress, the great white head turning. What did it see? Not food, surely, and not much of a threat, or it would have flown. Did it see us as fellow creatures? Or merely as drifting shapes, no more consequential than clouds? Exchanging stares with this great bird, I dimly recalled a passage from *Walden* that I would look up after my return to the company of books:

> What distant and different beings in the various mansions of the universe are contemplating the same one at the same moment! Nature and human life are as various as our several constitutions. Who shall say what prospect life offers to another? Could a greater miracle take place than for us to look through each other's eyes for an instant?

Neuroscience may one day pull off that miracle, giving us access to other eyes, other minds. For the present, however, we must rely on our native sight, on patient observation, on hunches and empathy. By empathy I do not mean the projecting of human films onto nature's screen, turning grizzly bears into teddy bears, crickets into choristers, grass into lawns; I mean the shaman's leap, a going out of oneself into the inwardness of other beings.

The longing I heard in the cries of the loons was not just a feathered version of mine, but neither was it wholly alien. It is risky to speak of courting birds as blues singers, of diving otters as children taking turns on a slide. But it is even riskier to pretend we have nothing in common with the rest of nature, as though we alone, the chosen species, were centers of feeling and thought. We cannot speak of that common ground without casting threads of metaphor outward from what we know to what we do not know.

An eagle is *other*, but it is also alive, bright with sensation, attuned to the world, and we respond to that vitality wherever we find it, in bird or beetle, in moose or lowly moss. Edward O. Wilson has given this impulse a lovely name, biophilia, which he defines as the urge "to explore and affiliate with life." Of course, like the coupled dragonflies that skimmed past our canoes or like ospreys hunting fish, we seek other creatures for survival. Yet even if biophilia is an evolutionary gift, like the kangaroo's leap or the peacock's tail, our fascination with living things carries us beyond the requirements of eating and mating. In that excess, that free curiosity, there may be a healing power. The urge to explore has scattered humans over the whole earth—to the peril of many species, including our own; perhaps the other dimension of bio-philia, the desire to affiliate with life, could lead us to honor the entire fabric and repair what has been torn.

If you know where to look, you can find ancient tokens of biophilia in the Boundary Waters. Downriver from the eagle's perch, we came to a granite cliff that was splotched with iron stains and encrusted with lichens. Paddling close and holding our position against the current, we could make out faint red figures on the rock, paintings that had begun to weather long before the first Europeans straggled through here in search of pelts. The pigment of ocher and fish oil had faded to the color of rouge, barely distinguishable from the rusty iron smears.

"There's a moose," Eva called, pointing at a blurry shape on the stone.

The rest of us agreed that the figure might be a moose, and we also agreed in discerning a bear, a bird, a beaver, a man or woman, a canoe, and, clearest of all, the prints of hands. What those pictures meant to their makers we could only guess. Perhaps they were hunters' icons, for worship and meditation. Perhaps they told stories or marked boundaries. Perhaps they were doodles. Without discounting other meanings, what I saw in the faint red figures was a group portrait, a way of declaring: Here are the people of this place, those that fly and those that go on four legs and those that go on two. The artists identified our human tribe by the upright stance, by the canoe, and by the imprint not of a foot, as for any other beast, but of a hand, that tool capable of fashioning canoes and drawings.

If one could paint such an elusive trait, our kind might also be identified by the urge that kept ten members of the human tribe paddling there below the cliff, studying those hazy shapes, trying to read our ancestors' minds, casting threads of meaning from our lives to theirs. Whether our interpretations were right or wrong matters less than the impulse that led us to make them. With nearly six billion of us now on the planet, and the web of life unraveling under the burden of our appetites, we need to foster in every way we can this countervailing urge to weave, to stitch, to bind.

It might have been my craving for a source of hope that persuaded me to see in the pictographs evidence of biophilia. Certainly I felt a kinship with those vanished artists, even as I sensed in their drawings their own feeling of kinship with bear and beaver and moose. If I were to mix red clay with fish oil and daub pictures on the granite cliff, I would begin with an otter and a loon, and when I came to represent the human tribe I would draw two figures, side by side, a father and a daughter.

❧

Although the pictographs are ancient by human measure, they are brand-new by comparison with the rock on which they were painted. As dark as charred bones, as gray as concrete, in places a dull rose, smoky pink, or crystalline white, the bedrock in this portion of the Boundary Waters was formed between two and three billion years ago, which makes it half as old as the earth and a thousand times older than Homo sapiens. How, standing barefooted on such venerable stone, and diving into the river for a swim, can one reach back through the abyss of time without losing hold of the icy, exhilarating present?

I swam each day of the trip, and each day the first dive was daunting. This was July, I kept reminding myself, and the otters frolicked here in January. Once I made the plunge, I stayed under as long as I could, eyes open to glimpse the otter's realm, mouth closed to protect myself from disease. Until a few years ago, travelers here could safely drink straight from the streams. But now acid rain has fouled even these remote waters, leading to the growth of *Giardia*, an intestinal parasite, and so we filtered every drop we drank and we sealed our lips as we swam. Once the initial shock of cold wore off, it felt good to rinse away the day's sweat. The water cleansed me through and through. After the swim, back in camp, where Eva and the other women brushed their long damp hair by the fire, I tingled for hours.

The day we paddled up the Horse River, several of us found ourselves swimming with our clothes on. The water was high from rains that had swollen the Missouri and Mississippi Rivers with five-hundred-year floods. Throughout much of its length, the channel spread out lazily into marshes of cattails and willows, but wherever it was pinched in by rock the current surged. The only way of maneuvering a canoe through the fiercest rapids was for one of the paddlers to climb out, grope for footing among the slippery stones, and push or pull the canoe upstream.

As I slogged through the first few riffles, I wore my life vest; but eventually I became so hot from the effort and from the midday sun that I decided to take it off, and I noticed the other waders doing the same. And so it happened that none of us was wearing a vest when we came to the last and worst of the rapids. Eva was in the bow of the lead canoe, and the man in the stern, the strongest paddler in our group, thought they could dig their way up through the central chute without wading. They made one hard run, then another and another, but each time they were stalled in white water and shoved back downstream.

At last Eva decided to climb out and tug from the front while her partner paddled. The canoe inched forward, foam brimming around Eva's knees, then her thighs, her waist, and when she lurched into the narrowest place, where the water pounded between boulders, suddenly her feet were swept from under her and she fell, barely keeping her chin above water by clutching the gunnel with one hand. The canoe spun crossways to the current and wedged against the boulders, and there Eva dangled, her face jammed against the upstream side of the canoe, her booted feet bobbing up uselessly on the downstream side. Watching her, I had the slow-motion sense from nightmare that something horrible was about to happen, and that I was powerless to intervene. I saw my daughter being sucked under and battered against rocks and tumbled down past me through the bruising rapids.

I *saw* it happen; but it did not happen. While voices all around me shouted advice, Eva clung to the canoe with one hand, worked the other hand free to seize the gunnel, then dragged herself across the roiling water and hauled out onto a ledge. Only the top of her head was dry. When I saw her safe, I realized that I had been holding my breath. I opened my throat, letting out stale air, but for a long while I could not speak.

Much later, after miles of winding through fragrant water lilies and gliding past the tranquil gaze of basking turtles, their domed shells gleaming in the sun like hubcaps, we arrived at a campsite on Horse Lake. Eva and I were to cook supper that night, and while she was unpacking the food and I was building the fire, she asked me if I had been worried by her dunking.

"I was terrified," I told her. "Weren't you?"

"No," she said. "It was kind of fun."

"What if you had gone under?"

"I didn't go under."

"But what if you had?"

"I would have washed up again sooner or later."

Recalling those fierce waters, those indifferent rocks, again I lost my voice. Eva frowned at her alarmist father, and we both returned to our chores.

Near the fire pit, where I knelt to fan the flames, stood a wild-cherry tree whose bark had been raked by claws and whose branches, glinting with purple fruit, had been twisted and smashed. Black hair dangled in tufts from twigs and paw prints gouged the dirt below. We had been instructed to bang pans or shout if we spotted a bear. We never spotted one, but if we had, I might not have been able to make a sound, any more than I could cry out when I saw the river snatch my daughter.

❧

There were dangers enough in the Boundary Waters. A few years ago, a father and son were pulling to shore when a black bear came rushing at them, seized the father, and began mauling him; the son beat the bear with a paddle until the father wriggled free, then father and son escaped in their canoe. More recently, two men dozing in a tent during a thunderstorm were electrocuted when lightning struck nearby and the juice flowed through roots under their sleeping bags; two other men in the same tent were only dazed. The week before our trip, a woman canoeing alone was killed when a tree felled by a beaver crashed down on her as she passed by.

We had not gone seeking danger in the wilderness, as sky divers go to the treacherous air or climbers to steep rock, but we had stumbled into danger anyway. We knew the risks of broken bones and drowning, the hazards from leeches and ticks. In the wilds, risk is the underside of beauty. To be a creature is to be vulnerable, to bruise, and sooner or later to break. Unlike most dangers in our cities, where guns or bombs or drunken drivers or heedless sex might kill us, what could harm us in the Boundary Waters had no will behind it, no malign intention.

The Horse River did not mean to hurt Eva, did not mean to frighten me, did not mean anything. Whether the browsing bear meant to wound the cherry tree is a harder question, but I suspect the answer is no. Whether the original world itself—the one that precedes and upholds our human world as ancient stone upholds the pictographs—whether the world means anything, whether it has a purpose or direction, is an even harder question, perhaps the most difficult of all. I do not pretend to know the answer, nor how one might be found, yet I find myself living as if the answer were yes. Arising out of a dead universe, evolving from simplicity toward unimaginable complexity, life does seem to be an immense journey—as Loren Eiseley described it—but one without a human destination. We are not the goal of evolution, nor are we competent guides, despite our tinkering with DNA. If we are voyageurs, then so are the otters and eagles, locusts and spiders, lichens and pines, along with countless species that have gone down into the earth.

While the Horse River was roaring through its boulder-strewn trough, the Mississippi River was drowning dozens of towns and hundreds of farms. Headlines described the Mississippi as rampaging, brutal, cruel, the same words we use for street gangs or packs of feral dogs. After we had spent so many dollars and decades to control it, how could the river turn on us this way? the commentators asked. How could it defy our levees, our concrete and steel? Cancers and hurricanes, earthquakes and the AIDS virus are often described in the same outraged tone, as if by shattering the walls of our houses or our cells they were violating some covenant between us and nature.

In defining wilderness as an unruly place where shaggy creatures roam, our language betrays an uneasiness about our own hairy origins and a regret that the world does not dance to our music. Beyond our campfires, beyond our tents, beyond our makeshift structures, the whole universe is wild, from quarks to quasars, from black bears to black holes, but far from being disorderly, it follows intricate, exquisite rules that we have only begun to decipher. They are not *our* rules, however, no matter how fervently we may desire to legislate.

Even such a remnant of wilderness as the Boundary Waters reminds us, at every turn, that we are not running the show. On our last evening there, the sky was clear, so Eva and I and two others gathered on a stony point beside the lake to wait for stars. Mosquitoes came droning in as usual at dusk, and the calls of night birds picked up as the calls of day birds dwindled away. A V of ripples caught the ruddy light of sunset, this time from a beaver, which carried in its jaws a stick the size of a baseball bat. The ripples arrowed straight toward us, and the beaver climbed out just below our point, so close that we could see its wet fur slicked back like a greaser's hairdo, and hear the scrape of teeth on wood as it gnawed bark from the stick.

I glanced at Eva, to share with her a conspiratorial grin. But she was lost in looking, and soon I was, too. By and by, disturbed perhaps by our feet stamping the rock and our hands flailing at mosquitoes, the beaver nosed away into the lake, gave the water a resounding smack with its tail, and dove. Moments later, it emerged again on the opposite side of our point, even closer to us, the wood still clenched in its jaws. One end of the stick was pale and shining, the other end, unchewed, still gray with bark. After a spell of gnawing, the beaver nosed away from shore again, smacked the water, dove, climbed out once more, gnawed, then reversed the procedure several more times, until we lost its movements in the gloom and lost its sounds in the stir of wind. Only then did we remember the stars, and we looked up to find that the sky had been covered by a quilt of cloud.

ॐ

The next afternoon, we slid our canoes out of Fall Lake onto the same landing from which we had launched them, closing the circle of our journey. Before getting on the bus I picked up a palm-size chunk of rosy granite, the edges sharp enough for scraping hides, and I stuffed it into my pack. I have often reached for the stone while writing these pages, turning and turning it, never quite able to make the hard angles fit my hand.

From inside, the shell of the bus seemed flimsy, the floor unsteady, the windows deceitful. My weariness alone made sense. Eva squinted across the aisle at me and said, "More and more like a bum. Now you could beg for change without a greasy blanket."

I stroked my beard, which had begun to feel like fur. "What do you think? Should I let it grow?"

"Sure," Eva said, "if you want to look like Father Time."

After a week away from clocks, I was beginning to hear time again in the whir of the tires, beginning to see it in the mile markers along the road. To keep time at bay a while longer, I hummed the melody from a song we had sung while paddling, and I shut my eyes. When I opened them again, rain was drumming on the roof and mist from an open window was falling on my face and lightning was cracking the pitch-black sky.

I was still watching the storm as we cruised through Chicago, the expressways deserted this Sunday morning, the street lamps a bleary yellow. The bus pulled in for a rest stop at a burger franchise near the Indiana border, and I made the mistake of going inside. The light and noise were painful, the surfaces too shiny, the smells too coarse. Everywhere I looked, mirrors multiplied the garish colors, the harsh lights, the feeding faces. Televisions suspended from the ceiling played cartoons, and at the tables beneath them diners shoveled in fatty food and sucked sweet liquids. On some other day, I might have sat at one of those tables myself, might have shoveled and slurped; but this day, this thundery morning, I backed away feeling sick.

Another day, I might have stayed there to admire the people, in all their shades and shapes; I might have listened to their accents and tried to guess where they were from. This was Chicago, after all, my mother's polyglot city, where my Assyrian grandfather practiced medicine among poor immigrants. But so soon after returning from the original world, I was not ready to see the human world as enough, not even in Chicago. Of course we should celebrate our own diversity. But we flatter ourselves if we think our rainbow of races, our preferences in making love, our flags, our ways of cooking and speaking and praying, our X or Y chromosomes make us more various, more mysterious, than all the rest of nature.

Back on the bus, Eva told me she had dreamed of looking out the window to see a great blue bird flying along beside us, a mighty beast with the crooked neck of a heron, the body of an eagle, and the fur of a lion. Mythology teems with such composite beasts. Eva's dream animal, in fact, sounds like a near relative of the griffin. While banishing griffins and centaurs and sphinxes from our textbooks, biologists have revealed that we ourselves are composite creatures, built up over millions of years from ancestral species, part lemur and part lizard, with bacteria in our bellies and mitochondria in our cells. Mountain and lowland gorillas differ genetically from each other more than we differ from chimpanzees. Does that make us indistinguishable from apes? No, but our genetic heritage does make us kin not only with apes and otters but with frogs and ferns and fritillaries—indeed, with every organism on earth.

The fellowship of all creatures is more than a handsome metaphor; it is a fact entwined in our DNA. The appetite for discovering such connections is also entwined in our DNA. Science articulates in formal terms affinities that humans have sensed for ages in direct encounters with wildness. Even while we slight or slaughter members of our own species, and while we push other species toward extinction, we slowly, painstakingly acquire knowledge that could enable us and inspire us to change our ways. Only if that knowledge begins to exert a pressure in us, and we come to feel the fellowship of all beings as potently as we feel hunger or fear, will we have any hope of creating a truly just and tolerant society, one that cherishes the land and our wild companions along with our brothers and sisters.

In America lately, we have been carrying on two parallel conversations: one about respecting human diversity, the other about preserving natural diversity. Unless we merge those two conversations, both will be futile. Our effort to honor human differences cannot succeed apart from our effort to honor the buzzing, blooming, bewildering variety of life on earth. All life rises from the same source, and so does all fellow feeling, whether the fellows move on two legs or four, on scaly bellies or feathered wings. If we care only for human needs, we betray the land; if we care only for the earth and its wild offspring, we betray our own kind. The profusion of creatures and cultures is the most remarkable fact about our planet, and the study and stewardship of that profusion seems to me our fundamental task.

While Eva and I were sorting the week's laundry in the basement at home, the good smell of mud rising from our jeans, she recalled her dream as one of the most powerful events of the week, and so I recall it now. Accounts of wilderness sojourns, like the sojourners themselves, often turn their backs on the human realm. Here is pristine nature, these accounts imply, and over there is corrupt society. Likewise, many who write about social problems, about poverty or prejudice or war, turn their backs on nature, as though we were acting out our destiny on a bare stage. But the stage is crowded with life, the stage is teeming, the stage is the main story. The only durable community is the one that embraces the whole planet, wild and tame. We need to find ways of speaking about that great community without drawing lines between nature and society, for such boundaries are just as illusory as the one between Canada and the United States, over which we paddled time and again during our trip without so much as a bump.

At any rate, that is what I am trying to find, a way of writing and thinking about the whole of life, human as well as nonhuman, in all its dazzling array. Although I am caught much of the time in ego's shiny jar, distracted by my own reflections, there were moments during our wilderness sojourn when I slipped out of that small self and entered, however briefly, into the great community. Those are the moments worth telling.

EARTH, AIR,
FIRE, AND WATER

ᣖ

WITH MONEY EARNED from helping neighbors gather hay in my thirteenth summer, I bought a colored poster of the periodic table, which I taped to the wall beside my bed. Before sleep each night, while my friends were listening to the rock-and-roll top forty or learning baseball statistics, I memorized the names and symbols and atomic weights of the elements. All of us were looking for some principle of order in the dizzy world. As my friends brooded on Elvis or Willie or Stan the Man, I murmured "actinium, krypton, zinc," trying to hold the alphabet of the universe in my head.

Chemists knew of 103 primary substances back then, from lowly hydrogen to weighty lawrencium. The makers of the poster allowed for future discoveries by leaving a few blank spaces at the bottom. And sure enough, in the fall of 1964, when I was a college sophomore, my physics professor announced that the Russians had produced element 104 in one of their accelerators. I penciled this news onto my periodic table, which I had mounted on the wall beside my dormitory bed, as a counterpoint of sorts to the pin-ups beside my roommate's bed. Within the next decade, along came numbers 105 and 106, but by then I had moved on in my search for order and was no longer keeping track.

ઢ

What fascinated me, during those years of sleeping with the elements, was the idea that all the dazzling variety of things, from starfish to stars, had been concocted from a hundred or so ingredients. Physics taught me a breathtakingly simpler view, that the elements were not primary after all, but were themselves composed from a handful of particles, such as protons and electrons, and these in turn were composed of even simpler entities fancifully named quarks, mere eddies in the cosmic flow.

Except for the change in vocabulary, this claim that the universe is made from a single underlying stuff was anticipated by Heraclitus twenty-five centuries ago, in his famous aphorism: "It ever was, and is, and shall be, ever-living fire, in measures being kindled and in measures going out." Other Greeks put forward rival candidates for the original substance. "All is water," Thales maintained, "and the world is full of gods." All is air, Anaximenes believed; no, no, Xenophanes insisted, all is earth. Then along came Empedocles, in the fifth century B.C., to reconcile these views by proposing that the cosmos is made not from any one substance but from all four, giving us the familiar quartet of earth, air, fire, and water.

The elements themselves do not change, Empedocles argued, but they are stirred into ever-changing combinations by Love and Strife, the one force drawing them together, the other driving them apart. These contrary forces are still recognizable in our notions of attraction and repulsion, positive and negative charge, particles and antiparticles. One of the central questions in cosmology these days is whether the universe will continue to expand forever, or whether it will eventually reverse direction and rush back toward the center. Empedocles might have posed the same question by asking which influence will triumph in the long run, strife or love.

As a devotee of the periodic table, I was at first inclined to scoff at the old-timers for believing that a mere quartet of elements could account for the world's variety. However, when I considered that only four kinds of taste buds—salt, bitter, sour, and sweet— allow us to enjoy an infinity of flavors, that all the DNA for the billions of creatures on earth is constructed from a series of four bases, and that all the motion in the universe may be attributed to four interacting forces, the ancient scheme no longer seemed so far-fetched.

Our science offers a much more complicated and, we trust, more accurate view of the cosmos than anything the Greeks imagined, yet we still rely on their twin concepts of malleable substance and shaping force. The more deeply we probe into matter, the less solid it appears; even if you could find a small enough hammer, you could not tap an electron. But at the every-day level of chairs and chocolate, the stuff of the world seems tangible enough, scraping our knees and teasing our tongues. Although we find it more plausible to divide that everyday stuff into a hundred-odd elements instead of four, in thinking of elements at all we are following a very old habit of mind.

For two thousand years, from the heyday of Greece through the Renaissance, sophisticated thinkers as well as ordinary folks throughout Europe and the Middle East imagined the world to be compounded of earth and air and fire and water. The four elements permeated the thinking of the early Hebrews, Egyptians, and Persians. Aristotle elaborated the scheme by arguing that every-thing below the moon is composed of the four elements, and therefore perishable, while everything beyond the moon is forged of an imperishable material he called "aether," from the Greek word for "eternal."

The Stoics maintained that fire came first, then air, water, and earth, and they predicted that sooner or later all will be consumed back into fire and the cycle will repeat. Modern cosmology envisions a similar possibility, an accordion universe, expanding from the Big Bang, collapsing back toward a Big Crunch, then expanding once more, on and on forever. Physicists no longer believe, with Aristotle, that any portion of this turbulent universe is immune to change; instead, they have replaced the material aether with a conceptual one, for they assume that behind the fleeting phenomena are permanent laws.

From the Stoics, the system of four elements was passed down by way of the Gnostics and Arab philosophers to the medieval alchemists, and from the alchemists to poets and visionaries right up into our own time. The old theory never really told us what the universe is made of, but rather how it moves, the way and feel of things. Earth is stubborn, conservative, and slow, with a long memory. Water is elusive and humble, seeking the low places. Air is a trickster, fickle and shifty. Fire is fierce, quick, greedy, and bold.

Over the centuries, these four characters have played leading roles in stories told by countless peoples. So Earth is the dry land that God separated from the watery beginnings. It is the mud brought up from the bottom of the primal sea by muskrat or loon, to offer solid ground where creatures with legs might walk. It is the dust from which we come and the dust to which we return. Water is the formless potential out of which creation emerged. It is the ocean of unconsciousness enveloping the islands of consciousness. Water bathes us at birth and again at death, and in between it washes away sin. It is by turns the elixir of life or the renewing rain or the devastating flood. Air is the wind that blows where it wills. It is the voice sounding in the depths of matter, the word made flesh. It is breath, which the Romans called *spiritus*, a divine thread drawn through every living creature. And Fire is the transformer, cooking meat, frightening beasts, warming huts, forging tools, melting, shaping. It is cleansing and punishing, flaming up from the sacred bush and lashing out from the furnaces of hell. Fire is a power given by the gods or stolen from them for the benefit of a bare forked animal. It is cosmic energy, lighting the stars, lurking in the atom, smoldering in every cell.

Turned over and over in our collective imagination, each element came to be associated with a color, a season, a number, a heavenly body, a point of the compass, a human temperament—earth is melancholic, air is sanguine, fire is choleric, water is phlegmatic—and each one accumulated an aura of metaphors. Late in the eighteenth century, while the French chemist Lavoisier was extending the list of elements to thirty-three, William Blake could write in *The Marriage of Heaven and Hell* about "The eyes of fire, the nostrils of air, the mouth of water, the beard of earth," and expect to be understood. Even today, when you pick up a bowl that has been turned on a potter's wheel, you hold the four elements in your palm, the clay shaped by wet fingers and dried in air and hardened in fire. And when you sit beside a lake—dirt or stone beneath you and waves lapping at your feet and wind blowing in your face and the sun beating down—you are still keeping company with the old quartet.

☙

Why did this theory spread so far and endure so long? Perhaps any people with a written language would eventually surmise that the world is made from a small number of ingredients just as words are made from a small number of characters. If the universe is an expression of the Logos, as the Greeks believed and as John's Gospel taught Christians to believe, then the elements may be understood as the alphabet of that grand utterance. But why four? Why not three or nineteen or fifty-six? Indeed, why do so many categories of thought come in sets of four—seasons, humors, cardinal directions, parts of music, ages of life? Why do so many symbols embody the four-sided square or the four-armed cross?

After long study of the alchemists and Gnostics, Jung concluded that a four-fold scheme appeals to us because it stands for our intuition of wholeness. "The idea of those old philosophers was that God manifested himself first in the creation of the four elements," Jung wrote in *Psychology and Religion*. "The four symbolizes the parts, qualities and aspects of the One." That root idea has been preserved in modern science, but with regard to forces rather than substances. Since Einstein, physicists have been pursuing the hypothesis that the four known forces—gravity, electromagnetism, weak and strong versions of the nuclear force—are descended from a single primordial energy, just as Heraclitus believed; and much current research is devoted to showing how, in the first moment after the Big Bang, the One broke down into Four. You can trace the old yearning for a vision of the whole through the pages of *A Brief History of Time*, where Stephen Hawking claims that by joining the four primordial forces into a single theory, we might achieve a complete model of the universe, and thereby come to "know the mind of God."

Although nowadays many scientists would be uncomfortable with Hawking's use of religious language, the great interpreters of nature have consistently used it, from the early Greeks to the alchemists, on through Aquinas, Galileo, Newton, Darwin, and Einstein, for they believed that in deciphering the laws of the universe they were articulating a divine intelligence. "Between matter as we observe it in the laboratory and mind as we observe it in our consciousness," writes the physicist Freeman Dyson, "there seems to be only a difference in degree but not in kind. If God exists and is accessible to us, then his mind and ours may likewise differ from each other only in degree and not in kind." Whatever language we use to describe it, the quest for a unifying vision is at the heart of religion and science alike.

Jung discovered from his own dreams and those of his patients, and from icons and myths the world over, that four-fold designs such as crosses and squares—especially those linked to the circular figures he called mandalas—symbolize the search for a center, outwardly in the cosmos and inwardly in the psyche: "The wholeness of the celestial circle and the squareness of the earth, uniting the four principles or elements or psychical qualities, express completeness and union. Thus the mandala has the dignity of a 'reconciling symbol.'" In this way, according to Jung, "the reconciliation of God and man is expressed in the symbol of Christ or of the cross." When the Romans inscribed "Jesus of Nazareth, King of the Jews" atop the cross at Calvary, they meant the title mockingly. But for the Jews who looked on, the initial letters in those Latin words would have spelled out the sacred tetragram INRI, representing the Hebrew words for earth, air, fire, and water. Thus a sign of mockery in the language of the oppressors was a sign of mystical union in the language of the oppressed.

I realize now that for me the periodic table was a mandala of sorts, a reconciling symbol, with its neat grid of boxes, its promise of order behind the world's apparent disarray. Gazing at the poster, memorizing the numbers and letters, I sought to hold the universe in mind, as though by grasping that outward order I could bind together a self that seemed always about to scatter like smoke. What I dimly understood, even as a teenager, was that the inner and outer searches were the same. I sensed that my chief business, beyond the daily scramble, was to discover what I could of the source and true dimensions of Creation, for in doing so I would discover the ground of this flighty, flickering self.

ಜ

The challenge for each of us, not only the physicist and philosopher, is to grasp the slippery world. How do you divide up this vast panorama into thinkable chunks? How do you speak of the parts without betraying the whole? The danger, for every sort of thinker, is a hardening of the categories; the danger is that we will take our metaphors literally, as though, by pinning our labels on the universe—ego and id, yin and yang, quarks and quanta, God and Son and Holy Ghost, the four elements or the hundred and four—we imagine that we have snared the universe itself. Any description of the world is a net thrown over a flood; no matter how fine the mesh, the world leaks through.

With that caution, and with due respect for the periodic table, let me return briefly to the lake I mentioned earlier—Wind Lake in northern Minnesota, to be precise—for that is where I found myself not long ago, listening to the music of the ancient quartet.

Late in July, I was canoeing in the Boundary Waters Wilderness with my daughter Eva and several friends. At our last campsite, on an island in Wind Lake, Eva showed me a spot along the shore that was hidden from the trail by a screen of hemlocks and birches, where an outcropping of dark volcanic rock thrust into the tea-green waves. Nearly as old as the continent, the stone had been smelted and harrowed and cracked, and every fissure brimmed with life—clovers and lichens, pale runners of strawberries, ferns the size of a baby's hand, fur of moss, spiky grass, spider and frog.

On a cloudswept afternoon that would give way at dusk to a full moon, I went off to sit by myself in that vibrant spot. Sore from a week of paddling, I stretched out my legs, braced my arms behind, and leaned back. Time ticked on, slowed down, then stopped. I grew still. Presently, like voices rising, the elements revealed themselves. The rock beneath me felt like worn bone—and there was earth. A stiff wind shoved kingdom after kingdom of clouds along the horizon—and there was air. The sun glared through every gap, drawing flames into my hands and face—and there was fire. Mist from waves beating on the stone cooled my skin—and there was water.

Now, I separate the four voices in order to speak of the moment at all. While I was sitting on the lip of Wind Lake, immersed in that music, I did not feel any division. I knew an utter fullness and wholeness that turns clumsy when spoken.

In our various alphabets we keep gesturing toward the One behind the Many. We are always speaking about the unsayable in terms of what we can touch and taste and see. That is the best we can do, as brief-lived creatures with only a few doorways of perception and a small but curious brain. Given our history, it is hard to believe we were not put here to *think* about this place, to ask questions, to gaze back at the source, as though to complete a circuit of intelligence. No single alphabet can express the full range of our knowledge. For designing a new molecule or describing the intimate behavior of atoms, the periodic table is far superior to the old quartet of elements. But for speaking about those moments when all our senses chime and we feel the harmony of the whole, the music of earth, air, fire, and water is still compelling.

WRITING FROM
THE CENTER

?●

IN KENYA, A man hungry for sweetness walks into a clearing and blows a few notes on a whistle. Soon a bird flutters at the edge of the clearing, chatters loudly, then flies a short distance into the woods. The man follows, carrying an ax. When the man draws near to where the bird has perched, it flies again, and the man follows. And so they move into the forest, on wing and foot, until they come to a tree the bird has chosen. If the man walks too far, the bird circles back, circles back, until at last the man discovers the right tree. He chops a hole in the hollow trunk and lifts out the dripping combs, gathering honey for tongues back home. The bird eats what the man leaves behind, honey and bee larvae and wax. So bird and man serve each other, one pointing the way and one uncovering the sweetness.

The bird belongs to a cluster of species called honey guides. The man belongs to a tribe that has known for generations how to summon, how to follow, and how to honor these helpers. No one can say how the cooperation came about, whether birds taught humans or humans taught birds, but it has lasted as long as the tribe's memory. Seek in a proper manner, these people know, and you will be reliably led.

For a writer, the search is more chancy. You cannot be sure what clearing to enter, what notes to whistle. Moved by nameless hungers, armed with words instead of an ax, you slip into the forest, avoiding the trails because so many others have trampled them, following a bird that refuses to show itself, a bird that may be leading you astray, a wild goose instead of a honey guide. You may never find the hollow tree, may wander lost for weeks or years, forgetting why you set out. And even if you do find the tree, it may be filled with bitterness rather than sweetness, and the bees may rush out and sting you. Still you wander the woods. What lures you? How do you know when you have found the hidden food that will satisfy your hunger? And if in a rare hour you find the source, how do you speak of it, how by mere words can you drag the slippery essence into light?

Setting aside metaphor briefly—only briefly, because metaphors are the elusive birds that lead me on—let me say as plainly as I can what I am seeking. I would like to know where authentic writing comes from; I would like to know the source of those lines that are worth keeping, the writing that brings some clarity and beauty into the confusion of our lives. I know all too well the sources of phony, forgettable writing—mimicry, trickery, exhibitionism, habit, reflex, fashion, whimsy, conceit.

But already in my plain statement there is a wrinkle, for who is to judge which lines are phony and which are authentic? The writer, to begin with, and then the reader. If you hope to write well, and not merely transcribe whatever drifts through your head, you must distinguish the honest from the dishonest, the deep from the shallow, by testing each line against all that you have read or thought, all that you have lived through. The reader never sees more than a tiny portion of what the writer could have passed along—and a good thing, too. Of the sentences that come to me, I throw away a hundred for every one I keep, and perhaps I should throw away a thousand; I wait for a sentence that utterly convinces me, then I wait for another and another, each one building upon all that went before and preparing for all that follow, until, if I am patient and fervent and lucky enough, the lines add up to something durable and whole. My business here is to say what I have come to understand, through my own practice, about the source and conditions for such writing.

ᐓ

In America, during the past century or so, we have expected worthy writing to come from the margins—of the psyche, of the community, of the continent. We have expected the writer to be a misfit, an outsider, a stranger in strange lands, uprooted, lonely and lorn. We have often taken moodiness, madness, or suicide to be evidence of genius. We have celebrated the avant-garde, as though writers were soldiers. We have praised the cutting edge, the experimental, the new, as though literature were a kind of technology. We have assumed that talent would either be born on the coasts or be drawn to them, toward the shining Atlantic or Pacific, away from the dark interior.

Literature may come from the edge, of course; but to believe that it comes *only* from the edge is a damaging myth, an especially beguiling one for young writers who are insecure about their background and eager for sophistication. In my own first attempts at writing I blundered far enough toward the edge to lose my way. I was born in the Mississippi Valley and reared in the Ohio Valley, deep in that dark interior from which writers are supposed to emigrate. In the 1960s I left the Midwest to attend college in New England, then left America to attend graduate school in Old England. When I began writing earnestly I was living in Cambridge, and I had the impression that true art could only be made far from the numbing influence of one's home ground, in exile and rebellion. Didn't Eliot, Pound, Hemingway, Fitzgerald, Stein, and

[150]

Baldwin leave the United States for Europe? Didn't Joyce and Beckett leave Ireland? Didn't Conrad leave Poland and Nabokov leave Russia? Didn't Lawrence shake the dust of England from his heels and roam the world?

Reasons for quitting America were not hard to find: the Vietnam War, the nuclear arms race, riots in the cities, squalor in the countryside, the cult of money and power, the blight of advertising, the idiocy of television, the assault on air and water and soil. England and Europe were just as tainted, I soon realized, but their ills were not my responsibility. I could live abroad without feeling called upon to join in the work of healing. And wasn't that the ideal writer's stance, as Joyce taught by word and example, to stand aloof from the human fray, paring one's fingernails, disentangled, free?

During my four years at Cambridge I wrote steadily and badly, in tortured sentences, about expatriates and drifters. In bleak times I thought of suicide—who hasn't?—and in genial times I struck poses. I learned the poses from biographies of writers who had scorned their home places, had leapt from bridges or boats, had breathed gas in rented kitchens, had taken to drink or drugs or dalliance, abandoning spouses and children, betraying friends, consuming self and others for the sake of the work, as though the poems or novels or plays were so many precious lumps of charcoal left from the burning of a forest. My posing never gave way to serious action, because I had no stomach for alcohol or betrayal. I knew that writers are supposed to be eccentric, but I could not force myself to go very far off-center. I could not persuade myself that anyone else should suffer for the sake of my writing. As it turned out, I could not even bear exile.

When I finished my degree I applied for a teaching position at a university in the south of England, and to my surprise I was offered the job. Teaching jobs were so scarce, the officials expected me to say yes on the spot, as I had every intention of doing; but when, at the end of a wearisome day of interviews, the chancellor smiled behind his rimless spectacles and put the choice before me, to stay there and make a career in England, I trembled and said no. For all my dismay over America, for all my infatuation with literary exile, I could not become an expatriate. The gravity of home was too strong.

On the train ride back to Cambridge, shaken by my decision, I began remembering the neighbors from my country childhood who had lost jobs, the discouraged men, the bruised women, the hungry kids begging food at school, patches on their clothes, rain leaking through the roofs of their shacks, hurt leaking from their voices. Instead of fretting over my own future, I sat on the train making notes about those faces, recovering those voices, recalling stories from the Ohio Valley, describing people and places I thought I had left forever, and in that way, ambushed by memory, I finally wrote a few lines worth keeping.

꒰Ꙭ꒱

Those four years in England were also the opening years of a marriage that seemed a wonder and blessing to me, as filled with trials and revelations as any trek to the Pole. Ruth and I had known one another since before we were old enough to drive. We had courted chiefly through the mail, exchanging hundreds of letters. The desire to impress her on the page with my flair and affection had given me the first powerful incentive to write well. It seemed miraculous that she had become my wife, my companion in daily discoveries, my fellow traveler. We looked forward to having children, buying a small house with a bit of garden out back, sharing work and neighbors, settling down. The country of marriage, as Wendell Berry calls it, was more vivid to me in those years than any country defined by maps.

So I was troubled when I came across Flaubert's advice to a

friend: "Stay always as you are, don't get married, don't have children, get as little emotionally involved as possible, give the least hold to the enemy. I've seen what they call happiness at close quarters and I looked at its underside; to wish to possess it is a dangerous mania." I could not imagine being more deeply involved with another person, waking and sleeping, than I was with Ruth, nor could I believe that made her the enemy of my art. And yet Flaubert's warning was echoed by Turgenev: "It is not a good thing for an artist to marry. As the ancients used to say, if you serve a Muse, you must serve her and no one else. An unhappy marriage may perhaps contribute to the development of talent, but a happy one is no good at all."

If those two crusty old bachelors were the only ones who thought that writers should be loners, I could simply have ignored what they had to say. But Flaubert and Turgenev were voicing the dogma of a sizable denomination in the Church of Literature, a sect whose members are mostly but not exclusively male. The dogma holds that if you are to be a serious writer, a writer for the ages, a writer to be reckoned with in the hall of fame, then you must sacrifice everyone and everything else to your work. Resist all other claims on your mind, your emotions, your loyalties. Love art with all your heart. Stand apart.

A writer need not be single in order to believe in the virtues of detachment. Emerson, for example, though very much the pater-familias, confided to his journal that "the writer ought not to be married, ought not to have a family. I think the Roman Church with its celibate clergy & its monastic cells was right. If he must marry, perhaps he should be regarded happiest who has a shrew for a wife, a sharp-tongued notable dame who can & will assume the total economy of the house."

Here the terms of the choice are clearly masculine: the writer should become either a monk, entirely devoted to the word, or else a literary prince, waited on hand and foot by the sort of helpmate whom Conrad, alluding to his own wife, called "a silent, watchful, tireless affection." The writer's wife need not be silent, Emerson suggests, so long as she not be lovable. Let her be a shrew, but a good manager. Then while the uncaptivating mistress runs the house, the master may compose in solitude, emerging only to deliver manuscripts or to pat the children on the head.

For all the masculine tinge of those pronouncements on marriage, there is more than male arrogance behind the yearning for detachment. Some female writers have imagined themselves as nuns, in the manner of Emily Dickinson; many have remained single, as did Jane Austen, Willa Cather, and Flannery O'Connor; others, including Kate Chopin and Isak Dinesen, have come into their own as writers only after the end of marriage; and a few at least of the married ones have turned husbands and children into acolytes. Women have had to tug harder and longer to open doors into rooms of their own; but the desire for such a room, for the uncluttered space of mind, for the freedom to pursue one's imaginings without restraint from any other soul, is neither male nor female.

In "Silences," a much-quoted statement about the conditions for writing, Tillie Olsen argues that "substantial creative work" can be produced only when "writing is one's profession, practiced habitually, in freed, protected, undistracted time as needed, when it is needed. Where the claims of creation cannot be primary, the results are atrophy; unfinished work; minor effort and accomplishment; silences." It would be hard for any writer who has tried juggling job and marriage and art to disagree with Olsen; and yet her argument begins to sound ominous when she sums it up by quoting Kafka: "Evil is whatever distracts." The patients of Chekhov or William Carlos Williams must have been distracting, and likewise the death-camp mates of Primo Levi, the friends of Nadine Gordimer suffering from apartheid, the students of Theodore Roethke and Denise Levertov, the war comrades of Tim O'Brien, the enslaved ancestors of Toni Morrison, the husbands or wives of other writers, the grandparents, the daily news, the hummingbird at the feeder, the violet in the grass, the rising moon, the great worrisome world with its needs and splendors. If whatever distracts is evil, then we are back to Flaubert's advice, that the writer should flee as from an enemy anyone or anything that makes an emotional claim.

Marriage means—in the usual course of things—children, in-laws, neighbors, mortgages, insurance, furniture, quarrels: it means being snarled in the world, being *answerable*. What writer, em-broiled in family and household and job, has never dreamed of stealing away into seclusion? What writer of either sex has not sometimes yearned, as Emerson phrased it, "to be released from every species of public or private responsibility"? No bills to pay, dishes to wash, deadlines to meet, no oil or diapers to change, no ringing phones or barking dogs, no letters to answer or drains to unclog, no one and nothing to contend with except the work at hand. Arts colonies thrive because they offer just such a release, however temporarily. If anyone out there has labored at writing without ever craving such freedom, please will your brain to science, so that we might discover the secret of your serenity.

Of course it is easier to make books if you are single, childless, and looked after by servants, especially if you also enjoy a private income. Yet Flaubert, Turgenev, Emerson, Olsen, and other advo-cates of the unencumbered life argue not merely that such a life will be easier but also that the fruits will be finer. They are saying that books made in splendid isolation will be superior to those made in the midst of family. If the family is afflicted with happi-ness, so much the worse, for joy will lull you to dullness. Do not go gentle into that delight, the champions of detachment warn us. Do not become entangled. Love nothing except your work, lest you confuse the Muse. Be single-minded, ruthless, aloof.

There is a seductive purity in that vision of the writing life, as there is in any life consecrated to a single labor. Yet for anyone who, in spite of Flaubert's caveat, cannot help being "emotionally involved," for anyone who relishes the moil of marriage, it is also a limiting vision. Thoroughly wedded to Ruth, I have never desired to become Ruth-less, neither during those Cambridge years nor at any time since. Nor would I, having become a father, choose to be childless, even though my mind and mood sway in the most distracting sympathy with the movements of my children. Instead of regarding marriage as a hindrance, I have come to see it as the arena where I wrestle with concerns that are as old as our species. That is what Gary Snyder means, I believe, when he speaks in *The Real Work* of family as "the Practice Hall." From his time in Zen monasteries and fire towers, Snyder understands the virtues of solitude; but he also understands the virtues of companionship. "I have a certain resistance," he explains, "to artificially created territories to do practice in, when we don't realize how much territory for practice we have right at hand always." The goal of the writer's practice is the same as anyone else's: to seek understanding of who and where and what we are, to come fully awake. If you are well married, sharing a life and not merely a bed or a bank account, then family may become your territory for doing the real work—spiritual as well as practical—of being human.

&

When I said no to the offer of a teaching post in England, it was a married man's decision, for Ruth had even less of a desire than I did to become an expatriate. As a scientist, she had never succumbed to the Romantic notion that creativity flourishes only on the margins, in wandering and exile. Nor did she see any reason why a person could not make discoveries in the middle of the country as well as on the coasts. So when I was offered jobs back in America beside the shining Atlantic and Pacific, Ruth persuaded me to turn them down in favor of one in her home state of Indiana, in Bloomington, where she had studied chemistry. Southern Indiana was in the Ohio Valley, she pointed out, so the people and houses and churches and landscape would remind me of the places where I had first paid attention to the world.

As soon as we unpacked our bags in Bloomington, I set out to explore the neighborhood, to learn its ways and wildflowers, to hike the trails, drive the back roads, listen and watch. I bought Geological Survey maps and traced the contour lines. I sat in on trials at the courthouse. At the farmer's market I found out what to plant in our yard. On street corners, park benches, and parlor sofas I heard local tales and songs. I read graffiti in the alleyways, gravestones in the cemeteries, gravels in the creekbeds. In dirt and rocks, in museums and books, I studied the history of my region, beginning with the ancient oceans, on through periods of mountain-building and glaciation, through ten thousand years of civilization by native people, centuries of European exploration and settlement, the clearing of forests, homesteading, farming, manufacturing, the spread of canals and railroads and highways, the rise of cities, right up to my own tumultuous time. In all these explorations, I was not following a literary strategy, I was following my nose—or, to invoke a more elegant organ, my heart. Weary of travel, I was glad to give up being a visitor and ready to become an inhabitant. I wished to make my new home ground the ground of my imagination.

The impulse to marry a place, like the impulse to marry a person, runs against the grain of much writerly advice. In *The Triggering Town*, to choose an influential example, Richard Hugo urges us to avoid writing about our own neighborhoods, and to write instead about strange towns, where we feel no "emotional investment," where we are constrained by "no trivial concerns such as loyalty to truth, a nagging consideration had [we] stayed home." As an outsider, a sort of literary tourist, you need be faithful only to your words. "You owe reality nothing," Hugo insists, "and the truth about your feelings everything." Surely that is an odd disjunction, to set feelings against reality, as if the writer's imagination were sealed inside a floating bubble. Hugo does acknowledge that "after a long time and a lot of writing, you may be able to go back armed to places of real personal significance." But by that time you may well have been confirmed in the role of literary tourist, one who wanders in search of material, as the strip miner hunts for coal or the timber cruiser hunts for board feet.

Whitman envisioned the American land as a patchwork of neighborhoods, but also as an expanse to be overcome. In our view of the continent, there has always been this tension between an attachment to place and a yearning to conquer distances. Our frenzied building of roads, our restless mobility, our taste for the standardized fare of franchises are all expressions of this anxiety about wide open spaces. The net effect of Whitman's rhetoric, if not his biography, was to glamorize the mover at the expense of the settler. Much of our literature is the work of earnest pilgrims, idle drifters, travelers who write from a distance about places they have abandoned, or nomads who write about no place at all.

I am more attracted by the examples of American writers who, sometimes after periods of wandering, have settled down and rooted their art in a chosen place: most famously Thoreau, of course, in Concord; Faulkner in his patch of Mississippi, Eudora Welty in hers; William Carlos Williams in Rutherford, New Jersey; Flannery O'Connor in Milledgeville, Georgia; Grace Paley in New York City; Wendell Berry on his farm beside the Kentucky River; Ursula Le Guin amidst the rain and rhododendrons of western Oregon; Gary Snyder in the Sierra foothills of northern California; Mary Oliver on Cape Cod. Each of these writers possesses a "locus of the imagination"—to borrow a phrase from the Dakota poet Thomas McGrath—and each one has engaged in a lover's quarrel with his or her place, seeing it critically in light of knowledge about other places and other possibilities.

Even though her white skin has at times made her feel unwelcome as well as guilty in her homeland, Nadine Gordimer has chosen to stay in South Africa, to use her intelligence and imagination in the struggle for a free society. "One thing is clear," Gordimer insists, "ours is a period when few can claim the absolute value of a writer without reference to a context of responsibilities." It is striking, how directly she contradicts Emerson's desire "to be released from every species of public or private responsibility." In an age of totalitarian politics and coercive mass media, those responsibilities include giving voice to the silent, upholding the integrity and precision of language, speaking truth to power.

By chance and necessity, Pablo Neruda lived in a good many countries, and yet, according to his *Memoirs*, he never let go of his native land, and the land never let go of him. When his period of foreign service and political exile was over, he returned to Chile:

> I believe a man should live in his own country and I think the deracination of human beings leads to frustration, in one way or another obstructing the light of the soul. I can live only in my own country. I cannot live without having my feet and my hands on it and my ear against it, without feeling the movement of its waters and its shadows, without feeling my roots reach down into its soil for maternal nourishment.

For writers who are firmly in place, the metaphor of roots is inescapable. "Nothing can grow unless it taps into the soil," William Carlos Williams tells us in his *Autobiography*. To put down roots does not mean, however, that one can no longer budge. Our legs were made for walking, as the heartbreak songs proclaim. But instead of walking away from our messes and confusions, as Americans have traditionally done, instead of rambling forever toward pay dirt or sunset, aimless as tumbleweed, we need to move in loops, out and back again, exploring our home ground, as owls or foxes or indigenous people explore the territory they use for hunting, gathering, mating, and play.

The writer who is steadfast rather than footloose risks being dismissed as regional or quaint. What could be more backward than staying put in a culture that rushes about? How can you see the big picture from a small place? I find the beginnings of an answer in the word *stead* itself, which derives from an Indo-European word meaning to stand. To be steadfast is to stand by someone or something, out of a conviction that what you are committed to is worth loving and defending. A homestead is a place where one makes a stand. A farmstead in the Midwest is typically a huddle of sheds and barns and silos around a house, with trees for shade in summer and for windbreak in winter, surrounded by hundreds of acres of pastures or cultivated fields, like a tiny human island in a fertile sea. Whenever I see those farmsteads, I sense the smothering isolation, but I also sense the gathered purpose.

Knowledge of how one's region fits into larger patterns is the surest defense against parochialism. "Being regional, being in place, has its own sort of bias," Gary Snyder concedes, "but it cannot be too inflated because it is rooted in the inviolable processes of the natural world." We need to recover the ancient sense of homeland as an area defined not by armies and flags, not by religion or race, but by nature and geography and by the history of human dwelling there, a habitat shared with other creatures, known intimately, carried in mind as a living presence.

The effort to know and care for and speak from your home ground is a choice about living as well as writing. In that effort you are collaborating with everyone else who keeps track, everyone who works for the good of the community and the land. None of us is likely to fulfill the grand ambition of Joyce's young artist, Stephen Dedalus, to forge in the smithy of our souls the conscience of our race; but we might help form the conscience of a *place*, and that seems to me ambition enough for a lifetime's labor. Trees tap into the soil, drawing nourishment and returning fertility. Capturing sunlight, breaking down stone, dropping a mulch of leaves, replenishing the air, trees improve the conditions for other species and for the saplings that will replace them. So might writers, through works of imagination, give back to the places that feed them a more abundant life.

ᶻ♠

By choosing to settle in the Midwest, far from the mythical cutting edge and the actual publishing houses, I made another unfashionable decision. Every young writer I knew in my wandering years wished to live in London or Paris, New York or Boston, San Francisco or Los Angeles. My friends asked me what on earth I would do way out there in Indiana. Whom would I talk with? How would I keep my mind alive? Did Hoosiers give a hoot about literature? Booth Tarkington had left Indiana to seek fame and fortune elsewhere, and so had Theodore Dreiser, Kenneth Rexroth, and Kurt Vonnegut. But what writer of consequence had ever moved there? At age twenty-five, a writer of no consequence whatsoever, I could not answer those questions.

I found little support for my decision in books. The most celebrated literature about the Midwest has been written by those who left— Mark Twain, Willa Cather, Sherwood Anderson, Sinclair Lewis, Ernest Hemingway, Wright Morris, Toni Morrison—and who made a case for their leaving. You can read variations on the case in *Adventures of Huckleberry Finn, Main Street* or *Winesburg, Ohio,* in *My Ántonia* or *Sula:* the Midwest is a realm of rich soils and pinch-penny souls, a country of raw farms and small towns and grubby industrial cities, populated by gossips and boosters and Bible-thumpers who are hostile to ideas, conformist, moralistic, utilitarian, and perpetually behind the times.

There is enough truth in this portrait for it to be commonly mistaken for the whole truth. Midwesterners themselves often accept the grim account, apologizing for living where they do, expecting culture to arrive from far away, like tropical fruit, and looking askance at anyone who makes art in their own neighborhood. If you were any good, they say to the writers in their midst, wouldn't you be somewhere else? Wouldn't you be living within a taxi-ride of the talk show studios? Wouldn't you be rubbing elbows with literary movers and shakers in those glitzy settings where folks move and shake? No offense, now, but if you were serious, wouldn't you abandon this homely country for someplace more inspiring?

Midwesterners buy the same environmental calendars that other Americans buy, we browse through the same books of landscape photographs, watch the same dazzling wilderness expeditions on film, and from all of those images we learn that real nature, like real culture, is somewhere else. Real nature means the sort of thing you see on posters—mountains and old growth forests, painted deserts, buttes, hot springs, volcanoes, glaciers, rocky coasts and white-water streams—and for scenery like that you have to drive a long, long way. The Midwest does not often show up on posters. It is a modest, subtle, working landscape. Yet even in this country of prairies and glacial plains and wooded hills, wildness wells up everywhere, in the midst of towns, inside closed rooms, within our own bodies. No matter where we live, the energy of creation flows in each of us, every second. We can feel it in heartbeat and dream and desire; we can sense it in everything that grows, from bacteria to beech trees, from babies to butterflies.

Since well before the Civil War—when Audubon began sketching birds along the Ohio River and Sam Clemens opened his eyes and ears to life on the Mississippi—the Midwest has been feeding the imaginations of writers. It has begun feeding their bellies in a more dependable way during the past few decades, as universities and arts councils have become patrons of the arts.

Only recently, however, in fits and starts, here and there, has the Midwest begun to nourish its writers with a sense of purpose, a sense of doing work that matters in a region that matters.

Many readers still welcome reports from the interior of other continents—the secret depths of the Himalayas, the heart of Africa, the Australian outback, the Amazon jungle, the Russian steppes—while neglecting reports from the interior of our own continent. The pundits who define literary fashion may continue to think of the Midwest, if they think of it at all, as the blank space over which one must tediously fly on the way to somewhere important. The blank spaces are not on the land, however, they are in our minds. Life struggles and blossoms and mutates here as it does everywhere. We will never know the whole truth, about this region or any other, but we could use a much fuller account of the Midwest than we have yet received.

If we imagine North America as Turtle Island, to borrow a metaphor from the old people, then out in the Midwest we are on the hump of the shell. Every bit of the shell deserves our attention. Some parts have been intricately carved and painted, filmed and photographed, rendered in prose and poetry, while many other parts have scarcely been noticed. The writer's work is to notice, record, and remember, to inscribe the shell with stories. The surest way of convincing your neighbors that they, too, live in a place that matters is to give them honest and skillful writing about your mutual home.

❧

To be sure, worthy books have been written in exile, in isolation, on the margins of continents, in the precincts of madness. There is much to be said for writing from the edge, and it has been said over and over. In our infatuation with edges, we have scorned the center, a word that carries for me spiritual and psychological

WRITING FROM THE CENTER

as well as geographical meanings. I am suspicious of theories about the writing life that urge us to abandon the common in favor of the exotic, the local in favor of the distant. The truth about our existence is to be found not in some remote place or extreme condition but right-here and right-now; we already dwell in the place worth seeking. I write from within a family, a community, and a landscape, concentric rings of duty and possibility. I refuse to separate my search for a way of writing from my search for a way of living.

Whatever the orthodoxy may be in the larger society, among artists there is a widespread belief that fidelity to anything besides art is foolish. Listen long enough to writers, and you will hear many of them chant, along with Yeats,

> The intellect of man is forced to choose
> Perfection of the life, or of the work,
> And if it take the second must refuse
> A heavenly mansion, raging in the dark.

But the choice seems false to me. One's work grows out of one's entire life, including—if those are the choices you have made—the pleasures and struggles of marriage, of fatherhood or motherhood, of householding and citizenship. Yes, in order to work you must withdraw, if only into the room of imagination. But you carry into that private space every scrap of your experience, however acquired.

The Romantic image of the writer as an isolated genius, inventing worlds from scratch, legislating for humankind—an image that seems to rule over much of what passes for "creative writing" in universities—also seems to me a dangerous illusion. We are the servants, not the masters, of words. Language arises from the long human effort to make sense of things, and therefore even the simplest sentence binds us to our fellows, to history, and, by what it designates and celebrates, to the earth.

[164]

ᎧᎠ

Early in my explorations of Bloomington I came across a limestone marker half buried in the lawn of the courthouse square and bearing the words, CENTER OF POPULATION USA 1910 CENSUS. When I read the inscription, I visualized a slab in the shape of the United States, with all the citizens of 1910 represented by stick figures, each figure in its appropriate spot, the whole array balancing on a point beneath my town. With the migration of Americans toward the setting sun, the imaginary point has kept moving westward. For a brief spell, however, the citizens of Bloomington could imagine they were living at the center of something, if only of a census map. The limestone marker was a pitch for importance, akin to all those claims one sees on license plates and billboards, naming this village a gateway, naming that state the heart of it all.

According to the historian of religion, Mircea Eliade, humans have always and everywhere imagined their town, their tribe, their temple, their sacred mountain as the center of the world, "the point at which the Creation began." So we have Mecca, Golgotha, Mount Olympus, the holy centers where profane and sacred meet. The very name of Babylon means "gate of the gods." The Lakota people can show you their sacred mountain in the Black Hills. The Hopi believe their ancestors emerged from an earlier, fallen world into the present one through a hole in their homeland, and that hole remains the source of all things. Depending on the gods we worship, those of us who descend from more recent immigrants to America locate our holy centers in Hollywood or Times Square, on Wall Street, Bourbon Street, or Pennsylvania Avenue, on the peak of Mt. Katahdin or the bottom of the Grand Canyon, on the front stoop or in the backyard.

The more geographers reveal about the earth and the more astronomers reveal about the universe, the harder it is for us to believe in the cosmic importance of any particular spot. Viewed from the moon, the grandest metropolis is only a molehill. The earth itself is no more than a speck of grit in a run-of-the-mill galaxy. And our entire galaxy, viewed from a few light years away, dwindles to the size of a struck match. If we fancy that our address gives us unique access to the source of things, we are only flattering ourselves.

None of us lives at the point where the Creation began. But every one of us lives at a point where the Creation *continues*. We ride on a powerful current, and so does everything else we can touch or taste or see. If the current were to falter, the world would cease to be. Because it is steady, because the order of the universe is so dependable, we forget it is there, as we forget the air we breathe. Spiritual practices are ways of recollecting and experiencing this orderly power. Zen sitting, Navajo chanting, Quaker silence, Hopi kachina dancing, the whirling of Sufi dervishes, the postures of yogis, the prayers of Muslims and Christians and Jews, countless varieties of meditation and song, are all techniques for reaching toward the ground of being.

Quakers describe what they experience in the prayerful silence as a "centering down" to spiritual depths, below the chatter and buzz of our normal preoccupations, and they speak of the insights that come to them, the words that rise out of the silence, as "openings." Both of these terms have helped me to understand writing itself as a spiritual practice. Ordinarily the mind is bottled up inside the ego like a firefly in a jar. The jar is cluttered with frets and desires, with calculations and calendars, with the day's doings and the night's fears. Our task is to open the jar, or let it be opened, so that a greater reality may come streaming in.

According to the materialistic philosophy that prevails in literary circles, the universe is an accidental collision of atoms, and the only reality beyond the self is the muddle of rival selves we call society, and art is an ingenious game played with empty tokens. But if there is a transcendent source, as I believe there is, then a literature of slick surfaces, private angst and social manners, of sexual capers and money-chasing and political intrigue, seems not only tedious but deceitful; it wastes our time; it scatters our attention; it fattens us on lies. Art that insistently refers to itself, to its own cleverness and importance, its own materials and procedures, seems petty beside art that points beyond itself to the great sustaining order. The ego is too small an enclosure and too feeble a source for enduring art; the social scene is too shallow. Unless you draw from deeper springs, the work will be thin and vaporous. "Why, thirty or forty skins or hides, just like an ox's or a bear's, so thick and hard, cover the soul," says Meister Eckhart. "Go into your own ground and learn to know yourself there." When we say that a person or a song, a story or a poem has soul, we are acknowledging the presence of more-than-personal meaning and power.

For one who senses depths beyond the self, writing becomes a centering down, an inward listening for openings in the stillness, through which authentic words may come. "I know no advice for you save this," Rilke tells the young poet, "to go into yourself and test the deeps in which your life takes rise; at its source you will find the answer to the question whether you *must* create." If the answer is yes, Rilke says, then "only be attentive to that which rises up in you and set it above everything that you observe about you. What goes on in your innermost being is worthy of your whole love." This may not sound all that different from Richard Hugo's motto: "You owe reality nothing and the truth about your feelings everything." But Rilke is talking about a level deeper than feelings. The depths to which he invites us, the depths from which the individual's life takes rise, are also the source and pattern for everything else. Find your way to that ultimate ground, root your work there, and you will have something worth saying.

Mystics report that every bit of the world radiates from one center—every cricket, every grain of dust, every dream, every image, everything under the sun or beyond the sun, all art and myth and wildness. If they are right, then we can have no more important task than to seek that center. Here is the honey, here is the slippery essence that eludes all language. We dwell midway between two infinities, of the unimaginably large and the infinitesimally small, and between the twin mysteries of birth and death. For better or worse, here we are, in a flickering, fleeting patch of light surrounded by darkness. We have no reliable device for pointing the way to the center of being, as the carpenter's plumb bob points to the center of gravity. We have no maps or birds to guide us there. We have only consciousness, patience, craft.

LETTER TO A READER

è♥

SINCE YOU ASK for an account of my writing, I will give you one. But I do so warily, because when writers speak about their work they often puff up like blowfish. Writing *is* work, and it can leave you gray with exhaustion, can devour your days, can break your heart. But the same is true of all the real work that humans do, the planting of crops and nursing of babies, the building of houses and baking of bread. Writing is neither holy nor mysterious, except insofar as everything we do with our gathered powers is holy and mysterious. Without trumpets, therefore, let me tell you how I began and how I have pursued this art. Along the way I must also tell you something of my life, for writing is to living as grass is to soil.

I did not set out to become a writer. I set out to become a scientist, for I wished to understand the universe, this vast and exquisite order that runs from the depths of our bodies to the depths of space. In studying biology, chemistry, and above all physics, I drew unwittingly on the passions of my parents. Although neither of them had graduated from college, my father was a wizard with tools, my mother with plants. My father could gaze at any structure—a barn or a music box—and see how it fit together. He could make from scratch a house or a hat, could mend a stalled watch or a silent radio. He possessed the tinkerer's genius that has flourished in the stables and cellars and shops of our nation for three hundred years. My mother's passion is for nature, the whole dazzling creation, from stones to birds, from cockleburs to constellations. Under her care, vegetables bear abundantly and flowers bloom. The Depression forced her to give up the dream of becoming a doctor, but not before she had acquired a lifelong yen for science. When I think of them, I see my father in his workshop sawing a piece of wood, my mother in her garden planting seeds. Their intelligence speaks through their hands. I learned from them to think of writing as manual labor, akin to farming and carpentry.

I was born to these parents in October, 1945, two months after the bombing of Hiroshima and Nagasaki, so I have lived all my days under the sign of the mushroom cloud. My first home was a farm near Memphis, close enough to the Mississippi to give me an abiding love for rivers, far enough south to give me an abiding guilt over racism. Across the road from our house was a prison farm, where I helped the black inmates pick cotton under the shotgun eyes of guards. My sister Sandra, three years older than I, taught me to read on the screened back porch of that house as we listened to the locusts and the billy goat and the cow. By the age of four I could turn the ink marks on paper into stories in my head, an alchemy I still find more marvelous than the turning of lead into gold.

My birth along the Mississippi, those forlorn black faces in the prison fields, and the country turn of my father's speech all prepared me to be spellbound when, at the age of eight, I climbed aboard the raft with Huckleberry Finn and Jim. That novel was the first big book I read from cover to cover. After finishing the last page, I returned immediately to page one and started over. From that day onward, I have known that the speech of back roads and fields and small towns—my speech—is a language worthy of literature. Nor have I forgotten how close laughter is to pain. Nor have I doubted that stories can bear us along on their current as powerfully as any river.

ঽ

The summer before I started school, my family moved from Tennessee to Ohio, where we lived for the next few years on a military reservation surrounded by soldiers and the machinery of war. This place, the Ravenna Arsenal, would later provide me with the title and central themes for my book of essays, *The Paradise of Bombs*. The move from South to North, from red dirt to concrete, from fields planted in cotton to fields planted in bombs, opened a fissure in me that I have tried to bridge, time and again, with words.

An Army bus, olive drab to hide it from enemy planes, carried us children to a tiny school just outside the chain-link fence. There were thirteen in my class, the sons and daughters of truck drivers, mechanics, farmers, electricians. At recess I learned whose father had been laid off, whose mother had taken sick, whose brother had joined the Marines. From our desks we could see armed guards cruising the Arsenal's perimeter, the long antennas on their camouflaged Chevrolets whipping the air. And in the opposite direction, beyond the playground, we could see horses grazing in a pasture and trees pushing against the sky.

Before I finished the eight grades of that school, my family moved from the Arsenal to a patch of land nearby, and there I resumed my country ways, raising ponies and hoeing beans and chasing dogs through the woods. On local farms I helped bale hay and boil maple syrup. Sputnik was launched in the month I turned twelve, adding to my adolescence the romance of space to go along with the romance of girls. I mixed black powder in the basement and fired model rockets from the pigpen, brooding on the curves of orbits and lips. Our neighbors were mostly poor, living in trailers or tar paper shacks, often out of work, forever on the shady side of luck. Several of those aching people, their lives twisted by fanaticism or loss, would show up in my first book of stories, *Fetching the Dead*.

Many of the adults and some of the children in those trailers and shacks were alcoholic, as was my own good father. Throughout my childhood, but especially in my high school years, he drank with a fearful thirst. Instead of putting out the fire in his gut, the alcohol made it burn more fiercely. This man who was so gentle and jovial when sober would give in to sulks and rages when drunk. The house trembled. I feared that the windows would shatter, the floors buckle, the beds collapse. Above all I feared that neighbors or friends would learn our bitter secret. The pressure of that secret, always disguised, shows up in my early books, especially in *Fetching the Dead* and the novel *Bad Man Ballad*.

I was not able to write openly about my father's drinking until well after his death, in "Under the Influence," the lead essay in *Secrets of the Universe*. As a boy, I felt only bewilderment and shame. Craving order, I hurled myself into one lucid zone after another—the chessboard, the baseball diamond and basketball court, the periodic table, the wiring diagrams of electronics, the graphs of calculus, the formulas of physics. I pitched the baseball so hard I tore up my elbow; I rushed down the basketball court so recklessly I broke my foot against the gymnasium wall; I scrambled so far into mathematics that I could scarcely find my way back; I searched the teeming pool under the microscope for clues that would bind together the tatters of the world.

&.

A scholarship to study physics paid my way to Brown University in Providence, where I spent four years feeling like a country duckling among swans. My classmates arrived with luggage bearing flight tags from the world's airports, wallets bulging with credit cards, voices buzzing with the voltage of cities. These polished men and women seemed to know already more than I could ever learn. My own pockets were empty. My voice betrayed the hills of

Tennessee and the woods of Ohio. My devotion to the abstruse games of science marked me as odd. Fear of failing kept me so steadily at my books that I graduated first in my class. I mention the achievement because I am proud of it, but also because I have still not overcome that dread of failure, that sense of being an outsider, a hick among sophisticates. Standing on the margin, I formed the habit of looking and listening. On the margin, I was free to envision a way of life more desirable and durable than this one that excluded me.

The public turmoil of the 1960s and early 1970s deepened my private confusion. Even though I am the least political of animals, during those college years I was gripped by one cause after another—securing full rights for women and blacks and Native Americans, saving the environment, ending the Vietnam war. All these causes seemed utterly removed from the bloodless abstractions of physics. I began to gasp for air among the crystalline formulas. I longed for the smell of dirt, the sound of voices, the weight of tools in my hands. I grew dizzy with the desire to heal— to heal my father and myself, to comfort the poor and despised, to speak for the mute, to care for the earth.

In this time of great confusion I began keeping a journal. I strung out sentences like guy wires to hold myself upright in the winds of uncertainty. In those creamy pages, I wrote as though my life depended on it—and in a sense it did. Gradually I found words to address the inescapable questions: Who am I? What sense can I make of this inner tumult? How should I live? Does the universe have a purpose? Do we? What finally and deeply matters? What is true, and how can we know? I was too naive to realize that worldly men and women do not brood on such imponderable matters. I brooded. I pondered. I haunted the library, cross-examined the stars, walked the grimy streets of Providence looking for answers. Here science failed me. These mysteries lay in shadow outside the bright circle of scientific method, beyond the reach of gauges or graphs. There were no diagrams for meaning, and I desired meaning with an unappeasable hunger.

Pushed by spiritual hungers and pulled by social concerns, I decided in my junior year at Brown that I could not become a physicist. Then what new path should I follow? I considered history, philosophy, religion, and psychology; but at length I settled on literature, which had been calling to me ever since my sister taught me to read on that porch in Tennessee. All those years I had been living within the curved space of books. I read as I breathed, incessantly. Books lined the walls of my room, they rested on the table beside my pillow as I slept, they rode with me everywhere in pockets or pack, they poured through me constantly their murmur of words. At the age of twenty I still did not imagine that I would make any books of my own, but I knew that I would live in their company.

&

Another scholarship enabled me to continue my study of literature at Cambridge University. I sailed to England in the fall of 1967 along with my new bride, Ruth Ann McClure. I had met her at a summer science camp when she was fifteen and I was sixteen, the fruity smells of organic chemistry lab in our hair, and for five years we had carried on an epistolary romance. At first we exchanged letters monthly, then weekly, and at last daily, through the rest of high school and all through college. Page by page, this girl turned into a woman before my eyes, and page by page I stumbled on from boy to man.

During those five years, Ruth and I saw one another in the flesh no more than a dozen times. And yet, after exchanging sheaves of letters, I knew this woman more thoroughly, understood more about her beliefs and desires, and loved her more deeply than I would have if I had been living next door to her all

that while. Even more than the keeping of a journal, that epistolary courtship revealed to me the power in writing. It convinced
me that language can be a showing forth rather than a hiding, a
joining rather than a sundering. It persuaded me that we can
discover who we are through the search for words. In composing
those letters, I was moved by affection for my reader and my
subject, as I am still moved by affection in all that I write.

Marriage to Ruth is the air I have breathed now for over half
my life. From the richness of marriage, its depths and delights, I
have learned the meaning of commitment—to a person, to a
place, to a chosen work. Outside of this union I would have
written quite different books, or perhaps none at all. To speak
adequately of our shared life would require a much longer story; I
have made a beginning, but only a beginning, in my fourth book
of personal narratives, *Staying Put*.

At Cambridge, once more I was a duck among swans. Once
more I felt raw and rough, like a backwoodsman trying to move in
the parlors of the gentry without upsetting the tea cart or the vicar.
Despite my good marriage, despite my success at Brown, despite
the scholarship that had brought me to England, I still needed to
prove myself. It seemed to me that all the other students were
entering upon their rightful inheritance, while I had to earn, day
by day, the privilege of being there.

For the subject of my dissertation I chose D. H. Lawrence. He
was another outsider, another scholarship boy, with a father given
to drink, a mother given to worry, a childhood divided between
ugly industry and beautiful countryside. I was troubled by much of
what Lawrence wrote about women, and I despised his authoritar-
ian politics. I grew impatient when he played the shaman or
crowed about blood. Yet he knew how it feels to emerge from the
hinterland and fight to join the great conversation of culture. He
honored the work of hands, whether of colliers or gamekeepers or
cooks. He wrote about the earth, about flowers and birds and

[175]

beasts, with something close to the shimmer of life itself. He knew that we are bound through our flesh to the whole of nature, and that nature may be all we can glimpse of the sacred. The dissertation, much revised, became my first book, *D.H. Lawrence: The World of the Major Novels*. Whatever it may reveal about Lawrence, it says a great deal about me.

On the sly, while pursuing graduate studies, I began writing stories. The earliest of them were clumsy and gaudy efforts to speak of what I found troubling in my own life—the Arsenal, the bombs, the black prisoners on that Tennessee farm, the pinched lives of poor whites in Ohio, my father's drinking, my mother's discontent, the war that was devouring my generation. The stories were clumsy because I was a beginner. They were gaudy because I felt I had to dress up my scrawny experience in costumes borrowed from the great modernists—from Lawrence, of course, but also from Joyce, Woolf, Gide, Proust, Yeats, and Eliot. I fancied that the point of writing was to dazzle your readers, keep them off balance, show them what intricate knots you could tie with strings of words. I suspected that real life occurred only on foreign soil, usually in cities, and among bored expatriates.

I was saved from the worst of these illusions through reading another modernist, a Mississippian like my father, a man haunted by the legacy of racism and by the sound of American speech. Faulkner inspired me for a spell to even flashier verbal hot-dogging, but, along with Lawrence and Mark Twain, he cured me of thinking that the life I knew on back roads was too obscure or too shabby for literature. Eventually I stopped showing off, accepted the material that my life had given me, and began learning to say as directly as I could what I had to say.

During those years in England I formed the habit of rising at five or six, to write for a couple of hours before breakfast, before looking at the calendar, before yielding to the demands of the day. The world's hush, broken only by bird song or passing cars, the pool of light on the table encircled by darkness, the peck of the keyboard, the trail of ink on paper—these became the elements in a morning ritual that I have practiced ever since. I wake early in order to write, and I write in order to come more fully awake.

A few of those stories, written dawn after dawn, found their way into British magazines, the very first in *Cambridge Review* in 1968, when I was twenty-two, then others in *Transatlantic Review* and *Stand* the following year. I suspect that the editors overlooked my feverish style for the sake of my characters—the Mississippi sharecroppers and Ohio prophets and Greyhound bus riders— whom they would never have met before through Her Majesty's mails. When I received my first check, I was amazed that a magazine would not only do me the honor of printing my work but would actually pay me for it. To celebrate, Ruth and I took these unexpected few pounds and went to see an exhibit of Van Gogh's paintings in London. By 1969 I was reviewing fiction for *Cambridge Review*, and over the next two years I served as that magazine's literary editor. My association with this old, illustrious journal, and my friendship with the young, industrious editors, Eric Homberger and Iain Wright, were crucial in helping me see my way toward becoming a writer.

With the change left over from my scholarship and with money Ruth earned as a teacher's aide, we traveled during vacations all over Europe and the British Isles. For me, these were literary pilgrimages, so that in Ireland I was looking for Joyce and Yeats, in Wales for Dylan Thomas, in Scotland for Burns. Inevitably, I saw the Lake District through the lines of Wordsworth and Coleridge, London through Dickens and Orwell and Woolf, the industrial Midlands through Lawrence, the southern counties through Wells and James, the western counties through Austen and Hardy, all of England through Shakespeare. I read Balzac, Hugo, and Sartre in Paris, Cervantes in Madrid, Kafka in Prague, Günter Grass in Berlin, Thomas Mann in Venice, Calvino in

Rome. Traveling with books, I came to understand that all enduring literature is local, rooted in place, in landscape or cityscape, in
particular ways of speech and climates of mind.

&

In 1971, I brought back with me from England a fresh Ph.D. and
a suitcase of manuscripts. The degree had earned me several offers
of teaching jobs. (I never considered trying to write without
holding a job. The unemployed men I had known while growing
up were miserable, humiliated, broken.) I chose to come to
Indiana University because it is in my home region, the Midwest,
because it attracts students with backgrounds similar to my own,
and because the people who interviewed me for the job had gone
to the trouble of reading my fiction as well as my criticism. They
wanted me to come, they assured me, even if I turned out to be a
writer instead of a scholar. Here I came, and here I have stayed. Of
course I travel; I spend months and even occasional years living
elsewhere. I hear the call of cities and oceans, mountains and
museums. But I keep returning to this terrain, this town, this
house, this work. The why and how of that commitment became
the subject of *Staying Put*.

Fidelity to place, not common for writers in any part of the
United States, may be least common of all in the Midwest. This
region is more famous for the writers who have left than for those
who have stayed. Samuel Clemens, William Dean Howells, Willa
Cather, Ernest Hemingway, F. Scott Fitzgerald, Theodore Dreiser,
T. S. Eliot, Sherwood Anderson, Hart Crane, Langston Hughes,
Kurt Vonnegut, Robert Coover, Toni Morrison: the list of de-
parted Midwesterners is long and luminous. You don't have to look
hard for reasons to leave. The region has not been very hospitable
to writers. Vachel Lindsay, who chose to stay and make his poems
in Springfield, Illinois, complained of "the usual Middle West

crucifixion of the artist." I think he had in mind the grudging, grinding legacy of puritanical religion and agrarian politics: art may shock Grandmother or corrupt the children; you cannot raise art in the fields or mass-produce it in factories, cannot sell it by the pound. Publishers and reviewers, most of whom live on the coasts, often regard the heart of the country as an emptiness one must fly over on the way between New York and California.

The message of all those departures from the Midwest is that life happens elsewhere, in Boston or Paris, in the suburbs of London or San Francisco. Some editors and fellow writers have asked me, directly or indirectly, how I can bear to live in a backwater. I tell them there are no backwaters. There is only one river, and we are all in it. Wave your arm, and the ripples will eventually reach me. For the writer, for anyone, where you live is less important than how devotedly and perceptively you inhabit that place. I stay here in the Midwest out of affection for the land, the people, the accents and foods, the look of towns and lay of farms, for the trees and flowers and beasts. I also stay from a sense of responsibility. Every acre of the planet could use some steady attention. I open my eyes on a place that has scarcely been written about. However great or small my talents, here is where they will do the most good.

ও

Those talents did not bear much fruit during my first years in Indiana. I revised the Lawrence book, which appeared from a London publisher in 1973 and from Viking Press in 1974. On the strength of my few, feverish stories, two senior Viking editors, Marshall Best and Malcolm Cowley, secured for me a modest advance on a first novel. I had been laboring on a novel called *Warchild* since returning from England, but I was at last able to complete it thanks to the generosity of Phillips Exeter Academy, in New Hampshire, where I spent the school year of 1974–75 as writer-in-residence. The hero was a young man suspiciously like myself: born under the sign of the mushroom cloud, reared on an arsenal, conscientious objector during the Vietnam War. In passing, the novel also chronicled the decline of industrial civilization and the death of nature. Thomas Mann in his late years or Tolstoy in his prime might have done justice to my scheme; I could not. In all of its innumerable drafts, *Warchild* remained a sprawling, operatic, rambunctious book. Just before I mailed it to Cowley and Best, Viking had been purchased by Penguin, and as a result the lesser contracts, including mine, had become scrap paper. After the gloom cleared, I realized that the world was better off with *Warchild* in a box on my shelf.

While at Exeter, in mourning for my botched first novel, I chanced to read the account of a murder that had occurred in 1813 in the northeastern Ohio county of Portage, where I grew up. A roving peddler was killed in the woods near the county seat. Suspicion immediately fell on the muscular back of a gigantic foundryman who had been carrying the peddler's goods. Two local men volunteered to pursue the giant through the woods. They caught up with him, led him back for trial, and assisted at his hanging. After the burial, three separate groups tried to steal the huge corpse. All this transpired against the bloody backdrop of the War of 1812, amid skirmishes with the English and the Indians. The conjunction of war and wilderness, a fearful village and a mysterious fugitive, set me thinking. The fruit of that thinking, begun in Exeter and carried on intermittently for eight years, was *Bad Man Ballad*, a novel that opens with bird song and closes with human song, veering from history toward myth. The concerns of the book are not so different from those of *Warchild*, for I was still trying to figure out how we had become so violent—toward strangers and neighbors, toward animals and trees and the land itself.

Reading in my haphazard way about the frontier period in the Ohio Valley, hoping to get the feel of history into *Bad Man Ballad*, I kept turning up curious anecdotes about the settlers. An escaped slave, a philosophical cobbler, a savvy farmer, a lovestruck carpenter would be preserved in the dusty chronicles on the strength of a single flamboyant gesture. A few of these worthies made their way into *Bad Man Ballad* as minor characters; but most of them would not fit. Unwilling to abandon them once more to the archives, yet unwilling to interrupt work on my novel long enough to write full stories, I began composing two-page summaries of what I found memorable in these frontier lives.

At first, I thought I would return to elaborate these compressed narratives later on; but I soon found them to be satisfying in all their brevity, with a flavor of ballads and folk tales, forms that have always appealed to me because they cut to the heart of experience. Over the next few years I kept writing these miniature tales in batches, until I had accumulated fifty, spanning the period of settlement in the Ohio Valley, from the Revolution to the Civil War. These were gathered into *Wilderness Plots*, a slim volume for which I feel an ample fondness, in part because it came to me like an unexpected child, in part because, although it was the fourth book of fiction I wrote, it was the first one published.

By now you may have noticed, if you pay attention to dates, that long periods elapsed between the writing of my early books and their publication. This is a fate so common for young writers, and so discouraging, as to deserve a few words here. The latest of the stories in *Fetching the Dead* was completed seven years before that book appeared. *Bad Man Ballad* took five years to reach print and *Terrarium*, my next novel, took four. By the time William Morrow gave me a contract for *Wilderness Plots* in 1982, I had been writing seriously for a dozen years, with only a single book of criticism to show for it. Dawn after dawn I forced myself from bed, hid away in my cramped study, bent over the keyboard, and hammered lines across the blank pages, all the while struggling to ignore the voices of my young children, first Eva and then Jesse, who clamored at the door, struggling to forget the well-meaning questions of friends who asked me whatever had become of this book or that, fighting against my own doubts. Every writer must pass through such seasons of despondency, some for shorter periods, some for longer. Each of us must find reasons to keep on.

What kept me writing? Stubbornness, for one thing—a refusal to give up certain stories, questions, images, and characters. The pleasure of living among words, for another thing. When I was in the flow of work, I felt free and whole. I played the eighty-eight keys of language as a musician improvises on piano, my fingers and ears captured by it, my body swaying. Although it is unfashionable to say so, a good marriage also helped me keep writing. I hid my gloom from everyone except Ruth, who stood by me in the dark, and who urged me to follow my talent, no matter how crooked it was, no matter if the world never took any notice.

➷

In the late 1970s, even while my books languished, my short fiction continued to appear in magazines, mostly quarterlies and reviews. For me, as for many writers of my generation, the magazines—with their underpaid editors working on shoestring budgets—have provided a training ground and a community of readers. In the years when I could but dimly see my way forward, I was greatly encouraged by a handful of editors—Roger Mitchell at *Minnesota Review*, Wayne Dodd at *Ohio Review*, Stanley Lindberg at *Georgia Review*, Robley Wilson at *North American Review*, and Ellen Datlow at *Omni*.

The final item in that list may strike you as out of place. Unlike the others, *Omni* is a glossy production, pays handsomely, and publishes science fiction. After exploring the past in *Bad Man*

Ballad and *Wilderness Plots*, I began pushing my questions into the future. Where might our fear of wildness and our infatuation with technology lead us? How far could we carry our divorce from nature? What might keep us from ravaging the earth? According to the arbitrary divisions imposed by critics and publishers, to speculate about the future is to enter the realm of science fiction. And yet, whether set in past or future, all my fiction interrogates the present, which is where we live.

Beginning with a visit to Oregon in 1978–79, and continuing for the next ten years, I wrote a series of stories that appeared in *Omni*, *The Magazine of Fantasy and Science Fiction*, *Isaac Asimov's Science Fiction Magazine*, *New Dimensions*, and several anthologies; and I wrote three speculative novels. The first of these, *Terrarium*, arose from a nightmare image of domed cities afloat on the oceans, all bound into a global network by translucent tubes. Citizens of this Enclosure would pass their whole lives without going outside, without meeting anything except what humans had made. Set over against this claustrophobic image were the green mountains and rocky coast of Oregon, where *Terrarium* was conceived, and where my fictional renegades would try to make a new life. I returned to this Enclosure world in *The Engineer of Beasts*, a novel whose central figure builds robot animals for disneys, the successors to zoos in those denatured cities. The central figure in *The Invisible Company*, third of my future histories, is a physicist who must come to terms with the lethal consequences of his own early discoveries, while caught in a technological masquerade inspired by Thomas Mann's *Death in Venice*.

As though I had not already violated enough boundaries by writing science fiction, historical fiction, criticism, fables, and short stories, during the 1980s I added personal essays, documentary, biographical fiction, and children's books to my profusion of forms. And why not a profusion? The world is various. Nature itself is endlessly inventive. How dull, if birds had stopped with sparrows and not gone on to ospreys and owls. How dull, if plants had not spun on from ferns to lilacs and oaks. Why squeeze everything you have to say into one or two literary molds for the convenience of booksellers and critics? Anyone persistent enough to read my work from beginning to end will find, beneath the surface play of form, the same few themes: our place in nature, our murderous and ingenious technology, the possibilities of community, love and strife within families, the search for a spiritual ground.

The subject of my biographical fiction is John James Audubon, a virtuoso who combined a number of classic American roles: immigrant, entrepreneur, real estate speculator, salesman, artist, naturalist, frontiersman, and man of letters. He was also a neighbor of mine, in geography and spirit, because he lived for a dozen years in the Ohio Valley and he formed his vision of wilderness in contact with the birds, beasts, rivers, and woods of my region. Although I have sketched a novel about his entire life, from the illegitimate birth in Haiti to senile retirement on the Hudson River, I have thus far been able to imagine freely only his childhood and youth, about which the scholars know few facts. *Wonders Hidden* follows Audubon up to the age of eighteen, when he escaped from France to avoid Napoleon's draft and set out for America, where his name would eventually become a talisman for the protection of wildlife.

I began writing for children in response to an invitation from Richard Jackson, founder and longtime director of Bradbury Press. He liked the narrative flair of *Wilderness Plots* and wanted to know if I had considered telling stories for children. Yes, indeed, I replied, for in those days I was making up stories nightly for my young son and daughter. Then propose something, he said. I offered to write my own versions of the tales that lay behind twenty American folk songs, like "Yankee Doodle" and "John Henry" and "Blue-Tailed Fly," songs my father had sung to me when I was a boy and that I now sang to Jesse and Eva. The result was *Hear the Wind Blow*, a book that runs the gamut from tragedy to farce, rejoicing all the while in our mongrel speech. Also for Bradbury Press, I adapted a pair of stories from *Wilderness Plots* to make two picture books, *Aurora Means Dawn* and *Warm as Wool*; and for Macmillan I have composed a series of tales about the settlement of the Midwest, including, thus far, *Here Comes the Mystery Man*, *The Floating House*, and *A Place Called Freedom*. Children are a tough audience, refusing to feign an interest they do not feel, and they are also an inspiring one, for they have not lost their delight in the play of words and the shapes of stories, nor their capacity for wonder.

I was lured into writing a documentary narrative by the quirks of my childhood and the accidents of geology. My home in southern Indiana happens to be surrounded by the largest outcropping of premium limestone in North America. Wherever you see gritty stone buildings the color of biscuits or gravy, from New York's Empire State skyscraper to San Francisco's City Hall, from the Pentagon to the Dallas Museum of Art and Chicago's Tribune Tower, you are probably looking at rock that was quarried and milled in my neighborhood. After a boyhood on farms and construction sites, in munitions loadlines and factories and workshops, I am drawn to men and women who labor with their bodies, using heavy tools to wrestle with raw, stubborn matter. So how could I resist the quarries, with their bristling derricks, or the humpbacked mills with their perpetual grinding, or the stone cutters with their shrewd eyes and skilled hands? In its original version, my portrait of these people and their landscape appeared with photographs by Jeffrey Wolin in a volume entitled *Stone Country*, and then my revised text later appeared as *In Limestone Country*.

Some years earlier, baffled in my work on a novel, I had begun writing another kind of nonfiction, the personal essays that would be collected in *The Paradise of Bombs*, *Secrets of the Universe*, *Staying Put*, and *Writing from the Center*. The earliest of these were straightforward accounts of experiences that had moved me—carrying my infant son up a mountain in Oregon, listening to owls beside an Indiana lake. Gradually I enlarged the scope of the essays until they began to disclose patterns in my life that I had never before seen, such as the confrontation between wilderness and technology in "At Play in the Paradise of Bombs," or the legacy of a rural childhood in "Coming from the Country," or the impact of my father's drinking in "Under the Influence," or the quest for the holy in "Wayland." Although grounded in the personal, all my essays push toward the impersonal; I reflect on my own experience in hopes of illuminating the experience of others.

ఆ

The challenge for any writer is to be faithful at once to your vision and your place, to the truth you have laboriously found and the people whom this truth might serve. In order to work, I must withdraw into solitude, must close my door against the world, close my mind against the day's news. But unless the writing returns me to the life of family, friends, and neighbors with renewed energy and insight, then it has failed. My writing is an invitation to community, an exploration of what connects us to one another and to the earth.

I love words, yet I love the world more. I do not think of language as thread for a private game of cat's cradle, but as a web flung out, attaching me to the creation. Of course the medium is constantly debased. Television, advertising, government, and schools have so cheapened or inflated language that many writers doubt whether it can still be used in the search for understanding. But knowledge has never been handed to us like pebbles or potatoes; we have always had to dig it up for ourselves. All of culture, writing included, is a struggle over how we should imagine our lives.

Stories are containers in which we carry some of those imaginings. They are the pots and bowls and baskets we use for preserving and sharing our discoveries. Whether in fiction, film, poetry, drama, or essays, stories tell about human character and action, and the consequences of character and action; by making stories and reading them, we are testing ways of being human. It seems idle to protest, as many critics do, that stories are artificial, since everything we make is shot through with artifice. To protest that experience is scattered, not gathered neatly as in stories, is no more than to say that seeds and berries are scattered, not gathered as in the bowl we have filled for supper.

Without venturing into metaphysics, where I would soon get lost, I need to declare that I believe literature is more than self-regarding play. It gestures beyond itself toward the universe, of which you and I are vanishingly small parts. The moves in writing are not abstract, like those in algebra or chess, for words cannot be unhooked from the world. They come freighted with memory and feeling. Linguists describe our ordinary speech as a "natural" language, to distinguish it from the formal codes of mathematics or computers or logic. The label is appropriate, a reminder that everyday language is *wild*; no one defines or controls it. You can never force words to mean only and exactly what you wish them to mean, for they escape every trap you lay for them.

Insofar as my writing is important, it gains that importance from what it witnesses to. I have written from the outset with a pressing awareness of the world's barbarities—the bombing of cities, oppression of the poor, extinction of species, exhaustion of soil, pollution of water and air, murder, genocide, racism, war. If I stubbornly believe that nature is resilient, that love is potent, that humankind may be truly kind, I do so in the face of this cruelty and waste. Without denying evil, literature ought to reduce the amount of suffering, in however small a degree, and not only human suffering but that of all creatures. Although we cannot live without causing harm, we could cause much less harm than we presently do.

The desire to articulate a shared world is the root impulse of literature as it is of science. Individual scientists, like writers, may be cutthroat competitors, out for their own glory; but science itself, the great cathedral of ideas slowly rising, is a common enterprise. Perhaps the symbol for literature should be a rambling library, to which each of us adds a line, a page, a few books. Whether one is a scientist or a writer, the universe outshines those of us who glimpse a bit of it and report what we see. Right now we urgently need to rethink our place on earth, to discover ways of living that do not devour the planet, and this need is far more important than the accomplishments of all writers put together. The health of our land and our fellow creatures is the ultimate measure of the worth and sanity of our lives.

I am forty-eight as I compose this letter to you. I have been writing seriously for twenty-five years, skillfully for about fifteen. Given decent luck, I might continue making books for another twenty-five years. So I think of myself as being midway in my journey as a writer. My steady desire has been to wake up, not to sleepwalk through this brief, miraculous life. I wish to go about with mind and senses alert to the splendor of the world. I wish to see the burning bush.

Writing is hard labor, shot through with intervals of joy. If there were no pleasure in the sinewy turns of a sentence, the bubbling up of an idea, the finding of a path through the maze, who would keep going? I feel the need to tell you many things for which there is no room in a letter, even a long letter. Nothing I have told you here can replace my books, which live or die in the minds of readers like you, and which bear on their current of words more meanings than I know.

WORDS OF THANKS

How could any of us write books without the help and guidance of many friends? I offer deep and continuing thanks to my Bloomington neighbors, my colleagues and students at Indiana University, and my companions in the Orion Society. I would also like to thank Jim and Deb Bushfield for leading me to the Boundary Waters; Deryl Dale for refining my taste in music and carpentry; Scott Jones and Rob Adrian for seeking to put my words on screen; Virginia Kidd for sticking with me; and, for nourishing me with their conversation, my thanks to Carol Bly, John Elder, Robert Finch, Edward Hoagland, Phillip Lopate, Barry Lopez, Gary Nabhan, Richard Nelson, and Robert Michael Pyle.

I am grateful to those people and institutions who offered me places where I could try out portions of this book on live audiences: Doug Atkins, Michael Johnson, and Jack Oruch at the University of Kansas; Ron and Cathy Baker at Indiana State University; Carrie Cadwell at the Roger Tory Peterson Institute; Robert Fox at the Ohio Arts Council; Martha Gehringer at Transylvania University; David Hoppe at the Indiana Humanities Council; Oliver Jones and Eleanor Kingsbury at the Ohio Humanities Council; John Kessel at North Carolina State University; Ed McClanahan and Jeff Worley at the Writers' Roundtable; Clint McCown at Beloit College; Dan and Ilona McGuiness and Barbara Mallonnee at Loyola College; Susan Neville at Butler University; William Nichols and Nan Jenks-Jay at Williams College; Judith Nichols-Orians at Vassar College; Mary Nicolini from the Indiana Teachers of Writing; Mary Rider and Norval Rindfleisch at South Dakota State University; William Schafer and John Bolin at Berea College; John Schultz at Columbia College; Carolyn Servid and Dorik Mechau at the Island

Institute; Kay Sloan at Miami University; Larry Smith at Firelands College; Frank Soos at the University of Alaska; Charles Wagner and Kathy Carlson at Franklin College; and Jon Manchip White at the University of Tennessee.

I am also grateful to the editors who have supported my work in recent months, especially Robert Atwan, Chip Blake, Jim Cohee, Stephen Corey, Terrell Dixon, Wayne Dodd, Ellen Dooling Draper, Emily Hiestand, Barbara Lalicki, Alane Mason, Donald McQuade, George Russell, Stan Lindberg, Eve Shelnutt, Scott Slovic, Larry Smith, Kerry Temple, and Deanne Urmy.

This book is dedicated to the contemporary writer who has taught me the most about living in place.

The people who have taught me the most about loving are those with whom I share my house: Ruth, Eva, and Jesse.

NOTES

BUCKEYE

5. Simone Weil, *Waiting for God,* trans. Emma Craufurd (New York: Harper & Row, 1973), p. 178.

BENEATH THE SMOOTH SKIN OF AMERICA

19. René Dubos, *The Wooing of Earth* (New York: Scribner's, 1980), p. 69.

IMAGINING THE MIDWEST

25–26. Alexis de Tocqueville, *Democracy in America,* ed. Richard D. Heffner (New York: Mentor, 1956), pp. 159, 119.

26. The full title of Dickens's travel book is *American Notes for General Circulation,* the final two words alluding to the fact that his books were routinely pirated by American publishers

27. Hamlin Garland, *Main-Travelled Roads* (New York: Harper & Row, 1930), pp. 81, 79.

27. Edgar Lee Masters, *Spoon River Anthology* (New York: Macmillan, 1963), p. 192.

27. Sherwood Anderson's remarks on sex come from his *Memoirs,* quoted by John H. Ferres, ed., *Winesburg, Ohio* (New York: Viking, 1966), p. 17.

28–29. Willa Cather, *My Ántonia* (New York: Vintage, 1994), p. 164.

29. Sinclair Lewis, *Main Street* (New York: Harcourt, 1920), pp. 108, 258, 290, 428.

30. William H. Gass, *In the Heart of the Heart of the Country* (London: Cape, 1969), pp. 178, 186.

30. Richard Rhodes, *The Inland Ground: An Evocation of the American Middle West* (Lawrence: University Press of Kansas, 1991), p. 104.

31. Wright Morris, *Plains Song* (New York: Harper & Row, 1980), pp. 124, 136.

32–33. Mark Twain, *Life on the Mississippi,* in *Mississippi Writings* (New York: Library of America, 1982), p. 293.

33–34. Garland, *Main-Travelled Roads,* pp. xi, 43–44.

34. Willa Cather, *O Pioneers!* (New York: New American Library, 1989), p. 54.

34. Anderson, *Winesburg, Ohio,* p. 245.

34–35. Lewis, *Main Street*, pp. 54–55.

35. Cather, *My Ántonia*, p. 227.

35. Gass, *In the Heart of the Heart of the Country*, pp. 172, 187.

35. Ernest Hemingway, "Big Two-Hearted River: Part I," *The Short Stories of Ernest Hemingway* (New York: Scribner's, 1938), p. 212.

36. William Maxwell, *So Long, See You Tomorrow* (New York: Knopf, 1980), p. 54.

36–37. F. Scott Fitzgerald, *The Great Gatsby* (New York: Scribner's, 1925), pp. 2, 118, 117–18.

37–38. Louise Erdrich, *Love Medicine*, New and Expanded Edition (New York: HarperCollins, 1993), p. 69.

38–39. Tocqueville, *Democracy in America*, pp. 140–41.

39. Yi-Fu Tuan, *Passing Strange and Wonderful* (Washington, D.C.: Island Press, 1993), pp. 178–79.

39. Garland, *Main-Travelled Roads*, p. 238.

40. Hemingway, "Big Two-Hearted River: Part II," *The Short Stories of Ernest Hemingway*, p. 231.

41. Conrad Richter, *The Trees* (New York: Knopf, 1940), pp. 179, 180.

41. Wright Morris, *The Field of Vision*, in Granville Hicks, ed., *Wright Morris: A Reader* (New York: Harper & Row, 1970), p. 397.

41–42. Lewis, *Main Street*, pp. 186–87.

42. Cather, *My Ántonia*, p. 3.

42. Cather, *O Pioneers!* p. 139.

42. Toni Morrison, *Sula* (New York: Plume, 1973), p. 152.

43. Louise Erdrich, *The Beet Queen* (New York: Holt, 1986), p. 179.

43. Lewis, *Main Street*, pp. 23, 31.

44. Cather, *My Ántonia*, p. 90.

45. Richter, *The Trees*, p. 261.

45. Tocqueville, *Democracy in America*, p. 181.

46. Booth Tarkington, *The Magnificent Ambersons* (New York: Hill and Wang, 1957), p. 186.

46. Louis Bromfield, *Pleasant Valley* (New York: Harper & Brothers, 1945), p. 103.

46. James Wright, "Three Sentences for a Dead Swan," *Collected Poems* (Middletown, CT: Wesleyan University Press, 1971), p. 156.

46. Morris, *Plains Song*, pp. 199–200.

46. Carol Bly, *Backbone* (Minneapolis: Milkweed, 1985), p. 19.

46–47. Gass, *In the Heart of the Heart of the Country*, p. 189.

47. Morrison, *Sula*, p. 3.

47. Paul Gruchow, "Rosewood Township," in Michael Martone, ed., *Townships* (Iowa City: University of Iowa Press, 1992), p. 81.

47. Jane Smiley, *A Thousand Acres* (New York: Knopf, 1991), pp. 4, 368.

48. Maxwell, *So Long, See You Tomorrow*, p. 57.

48. Cather, *My Ántonia*, pp. 11–12, 227.
49. *Wright Morris: A Reader*, p. x.
50. Cather, *My Ántonia*, pp. 197–98.
50. Sue Hubbell, *A Country Year: Living the Questions* (New York: Perennial, 1986), p. 141.
50–51. Carol Bly, *The Tomcat's Wife* (New York: HarperCollins, 1991), p. 79, and *Backbone*, p. 75.
51. Susan Neville, *Indiana Winter* (Bloomington: Indiana University Press, 1994), pp. 102–103.

SANCTUARY

62. *Meister Eckhart, a Modern Translation*, trans. Raymond B. Blakney (New York: Harper & Brothers, 1941), p. 148.
63. D. H. Lawrence, "Snake," *The Complete Poems of D. H. Lawrence*, ed. Vivian de Sola Pinto and F. Warren Roberts (New York: Viking, 1971), pp. 349–51.

THE COMMON LIFE

75. Alexis de Tocqueville, *Democracy in America*, ed. Richard D. Heffner (New York: Mentor, 1956), p. 278.
77. Tocqueville, *Democracy in America*, pp. 199, 67–68.
81. John G. Neihardt, *Black Elk Speaks* (Lincoln: University of Nebraska Press, 1979), p. 204. Neihardt translated Black Elk's words rather freely; however embellished they may be, these lines do express a central conviction of Lakota culture.
84. Aldo Leopold, *A Sand County Almanac* (New York: Ballantine, 1970), pp. xviii–xix.

FAITH AND WORK

96. Thomas Merton, Introduction to *Religion in Wood: A Book of Shaker Furniture*, by Edward Deming Andrews and Faith Andrews (Bloomington: Indiana University Press, 1966), p. xi.
96. Mother Ann Lee is quoted in Amy Stechler Burns and Ken Burns, *The Shakers* (New York: Portland House, n.d.), p. 75.

THE WRITER IN THE UNIVERSITY

98. Donald Hall, "Poetry and Ambition," *The Kenyon Review*, New Series 5, No. 4 (Fall 1983), p. 100.

98–99. Vladimir Nabokov, *Lectures on Literature*, ed. Fredson Bowers (New York: Harcourt, 1980), pp. 64, 350, 283.

99. Jean-Paul Sartre, *What Is Literature?* trans. Bernard Frechtman (New York: Harper & Row, 1965), p. 156.

100. John Barth, *The Friday Book* (New York: Putnam's, 1984), p. 108.

100. Rust Hills, "How Writers Live Today," *Esquire*, August 1984, p. 39.

101. Flannery O'Connor, *Mystery and Manners* (New York: Farrar, 1961), p. 86.

101. Denise Levertov, *The Poet in the World* (New York: New Directions, 1973), p. 175.

101–102. William Gass, "A Failing Grade for the Present Tense," *New York Times Book Review*, 11 October 1987, p. 32.

102. Hall, "Poetry and Ambition," p. 154.

102. Richard Hugo, *The Triggering Town* (New York: Norton, 1979), p. 57.

102. Gass, "A Failing Grade for the Present Tense," p. 38; ellipsis in original.

102. Eve Shelnutt, "Notes from a Cell: Creative Writing Programs in Isolation," *AWP Chronicle*, February 1990, pp. 1, 4, 11.

103. Hall, "Poetry and Ambition," p. 100.

104. Theodore Roethke, *On the Poet and His Craft*, ed. Frank J. Mills, Jr. (Seattle: University of Washington Press, 1965), pp. 96, 98.

104. Elizabeth Bishop, "Bishop," *Writers at Work: The Paris Review Interviews*, 6th series, ed. George Plimpton (New York: Viking, 1984), p. 134.

105. Levertov, *The Poet in the World*, p. 184.

105. George Orwell, "Inside the Whale," *The Collected Essays, Journalism and Letters of George Orwell*, vol. 1, ed. Sonia Orwell and Ian Angus (New York: Harcourt, 1968), p. 496.

105. E. L. Doctorow, "Doctorow," *Writers at Work: The Paris Review Interviews*, 8th series, ed. George Plimpton (New York: Viking, 1988), p. 318.

105–106. O'Connor, *Mystery and Manners*, p. 84.

106. Orwell, "Inside the Whale," p. 521.

107. Doctorow, "Doctorow," pp. 309–10.

107. John Gardner, *On Becoming a Novelist* (New York: Harper & Row, 1983), p. 36.

108. Terry Eagleton, *The Significance of Theory* (Oxford: Blackwell, 1990), pp. 25–26.

108. Toni Morrison, "Writers Together," *The Nation*, 24 October 1981, p. 397.

109. Patrick Parrinder, *The Failure of Theory* (Brighton, England: Harvester, 1987), p. ix.

109. Ezra Pound, *Literary Essays of Ezra Pound*, ed. T. S. Eliot (London: Faber, 1954), p. 4.

109. Sartre, *What Is Literature?* p. 22.

109–110. William Faulkner, "Faulkner," *Writers at Work: The Paris Review Interviews*, ed. Malcolm Cowley (New York: Viking, 1959), pp. 137–38.

110. John Cheever, "Cheever," *Writers at Work: The Paris Review Interviews*, 5th series, ed. George Plimpton (New York: Viking, 1981), p. 122.

110. Primo Levi, *Other People's Trades*, trans. Raymond Rosenthal (New York: Summit, 1989), p. 174.

111. Robert Scholes, *Protocols of Reading* (New Haven: Yale University Press, 1989), p. 60.

112. Wayne Booth, *The Company We Keep: An Ethics of Fiction* (Berkeley: University of California Press, 1988), p. 136.

112-113. William Styron, "Styron," *Writers at Work: The Paris Review Interviews*, ed. Malcolm Cowley (New York: Viking, 1959), p. 270.

113-114. Jorge Luis Borges, *Borges on Writing*, ed. Norman Thomas di Giovanni, Daniel Halpern, and Frank MacShane (New York: Dutton, 1973), pp. 165, 93, 91.

114. O'Connor, *Mystery and Manners*, p. 101.

114. Pound, *Literary Essays of Ezra Pound*, p. 91.

114. Annie Dillard, *Living by Fiction* (New York: Harper & Row, 1982), pp. 78–79.

114-115. Italo Calvino, *Six Memos for the Next Millennium*, trans. Patrick Creagh (Cambridge: Harvard University Press, 1988), p. 26.

115. Gary Snyder, *The Real Work: Interviews & Talks, 1964–79*, ed. William Scott McLean (New York: New Directions, 1980), p. 62.

VOYAGEURS

121. Olivia Ladd Gilliam, who died while I was writing this essay, brought an exuberant spirit and exquisite vision to the work of *Orion* magazine for a decade. Her devotion to art, to language, and to friends inspired many, many of us to work harder on behalf of the earth.

122. Our fellow travelers were Jim and Deb Bushfield, Jerri Hawkins, Jack Woodruff, Cathy Moesner, Terry Adkins, Barb Stembel, and Tony Steele, all boon companions.

127. Henry David Thoreau, *Walden*, ed. J. Lyndon Shanley (Princeton: Princeton University Press, 1973), p. 10.

128. Edward O. Wilson, *Biophilia* (Cambridge: Harvard University Press, 1984), p. 1.

EARTH, AIR, FIRE, AND WATER

144. Carl Jung, *Psychology and Religion* (New Haven: Yale University Press, 1938), pp. 70–71.

144. Stephen Hawking, *A Brief History of Time* (New York: Bantam, 1988), p. 175.

144. Freeman Dyson, *Infinite in All Directions* (New York: Harper & Row, 1988), p. 8.

145. Jung, *Psychology and Religion*, p. 96.

WRITING FROM THE CENTER

153. The remarks by Flaubert and Turgenev both come from Barbara Beaumont, ed., *Flaubert & Turgenev: A Friendship in Letters* (New York: Fromm, 1987), p. 17.

153. A. W. Plumstead and Harrison Hayford, eds., *The Journals and Miscellaneous Notebooks of Ralph Waldo Emerson*, Vol. VII: 1838–1842 (Cambridge: Harvard University Press, 1969), p. 420.

154. Tillie Olsen, "Silences," *Ms.*, September 1978, p. 99.

155. Plumstead and Hayford, eds., *Journals and Miscellaneous Notebooks of Ralph Waldo Emerson*, p. 420.

156. Gary Snyder, *The Real Work: Interviews & Talks, 1964–79*, ed. William Scott McLean (New York: New Directions, 1980), p. 106.

157–158. Richard Hugo, *The Triggering Town* (New York: Norton, 1979), pp. 12, 6, 18.

158. Mark Minz, "Poetry and Place: An Interview with Thomas McGrath," in John Judson, ed., *Voyages to the Inland Sea*, no. 3 (LaCrosse: University of Wisconsin Press, 1973), p. 40.

159. Nadine Gordimer, *The Essential Gesture: Writing, Politics and Places* (New York: Knopf, 1988), p. 288.

159. Pablo Neruda, *Memoirs*, trans. Hardie St. Martin (New York: Farrar, 1977), p. 165.

159. William Carlos Williams, *The Autobiography* (New York: New Directions, 1951), p. 334.

160. Gary Snyder, *The Practice of the Wild* (San Francisco: North Point, 1990), p. 64.

164. William Butler Yeats, "The Choice," *The Collected Poems* (London: Macmillan, 1965), p. 278.

165. Mircea Eliade, *Cosmos and History: The Myth of the Eternal Return* (New York: Harper & Row, 1959), p. 16.

167. Meister Eckhart is quoted in Aldous Huxley, *The Perennial Philosophy* (New York: Harper & Brothers, 1945), p. 162.

167. Rainer Maria Rilke, *Letters to a Young Poet*, trans. M. D. Herter Norton (New York: Norton, 1954), pp. 20, 46–47.

Scott Russell Sanders is a Professor of English at
Indiana University, Bloomington. He has published
numerous other books—fiction, nonfiction,
and books for children.